Memories of Steam

from

GLASGOW TO ABERDEEN

Michael S. Welch

with an Introduction by Tony Davies

Following a shower of rain, the track work and platform surface glis̶t̶e̶n̶ ̶i̶n̶ ̶t̶h̶e̶ sunshine as BR Standard 'Clan' Pacific No. 72006, *Clan Mackenzie,* pulls out of Gleneagles hauling the 9.25am *ex*-Crewe on the last stage of its journey to Perth. This photograph was taken on 28th August 1964.
P. S. Leavens

First Published by Runpast Publications 1993

Reprinted January 2012 by Booklaw Publications, 382 Carlton Hill, Nottingham, NG4 1JA

Printed by The Amadeus Press, Cleckheaton, West Yorkshire, BD19 4TQ

CONTENTS

A batch of BR Standard Caprotti 4-6-0s was allocated to St. Rollox shed when new in 1957 and these locomotives performed excellently on the Glasgow-Dundee/Aberdeen routes. Here No. 73151 is seen passing its home depot in charge of the lengthy 10.0am Dundee West-Glasgow train on 1st May 1962. *W. S. Sellar*

PREFACE

When I reflect on my experiences of BR steam my overwhelming feeling is that I was simply born too late to see the best. I was only eight years old when the Modernisation Plan was announced, but by the time I had left school and started 'chasing' steam in earnest diesels were already in charge of most main line passenger trains with steam being banished from huge tracts of the country. Those locomotives which remained were in increasingly run-down condition and I will always remember the classic words of a BR motive power superintendent, quoted in the railway press, who said the locomotives in his area 'were kept going with string and a prayer'. That certainly seemed an apt statement which just about summed up the desperate plight of much BR steam traction in the mid-1960s. I greatly regretted that I had missed the so-called 'glorious years'. Ten years earlier the BR scene offered a feast for the steam enthusiast but I had to make do with leftovers! Wherever I went the locomotives nearly always seemed to be indescribably filthy and the semi-derelict sheds in which the locomotives were maintained often seemed to be in worse condition than the engines themselves.

Of course, there were exceptions to this generally depressing picture, the exploits of Leeds Holbeck shed's 'Jubilee' 4-6-0s and usually sparkling condition of Salisbury's Bulleid Pacifics spring immediately to mind, but for me the undoubted highlight of BR steam's twilight years was the four and a half year reign of the Gresley Class A4 Pacifics on the Glasgow to Aberdeen three hour trains. On this route it was a refreshing change to find a fair proportion of the passenger engines kept in clean condition. Despite Scottish Region's repeated attempts to oust steam from these services there was a degree of commitment to maintain the Class A4s in reasonable condition using the heavy repair facilities still available at Cowlairs, Darlington and Inverurie works.

Thankfully the A4s were not subjected to the apparent policy of decay and neglect which seemed to be so prevalent throughout the other areas where steam survived and right up to the end were still capable of performances worthy of the class during its heyday, though it must be said that train loads were modest compared to East Coast expresses. I would certainly like to think that sentiment was not a factor in steam traction's survival on the Aberdeen road long after other principal Scottish lines had succumbed to dieselisation, and that the A4s remained first choice motive power due to their speed and general reliability. Certainly the latter quality is one which the diesels of the time noticeably lacked!

In this album I have attempted to portray everyday scenes on the Glasgow to Aberdeen routes during almost twenty years of BR steam from 1948 to 1967. Generally the routes were not as widely photographed as other, more scenic Scottish lines, and it was not until the mid-1960s that the lines received much attention from railway photographers. The Class A4s acted like magnets, attracting followers of steam from the length and breadth of Great Britain, who wished to photograph and travel behind the last of Sir Nigel Gresley's streamlined masterpieces. Consequently many of the photographs feature A4s, and most were taken during the final three years of steam activity on the line, which will be best remembered by the majority of enthusiasts. Originally I had hoped to include some pictorial coverage of each of the branch lines which are associated with the Aberdeen lines, but many of these were closed in the 1950s and I have been unable to trace sufficient material to do them justice. I have, however, decided to include the Bridge of Dun to Brechin and Montrose to Inverbervie lines both of which remained open to freight traffic for some years and for which I was able to obtain a reasonable selection of photographs. I have also included a short historical summary for each section of the route which provides basic information regarding opening dates etc.

I would like to thank my publisher, Stephen Mourton, of Runpast Publishing for allowing me control of the choice of the illustrations and layout. The Glasgow to Aberdeen lines were among the last in Great Britain where steam traction was maintained in good fettle and regularly rostered for demanding long distance high speed passenger turns, and so occupy a special place in the history books. This is not a history book however, but an album of photographs from which I trust readers will derive much enjoyment. If this volume provides readers with as much pleasure as I have obtained compiling it then my efforts will have been worthwhile.

M.S.W.
Burgess Hill, West Sussex
June 1993

Class J37 0-6-0 No. 64611 potters along the Brechin branch with a freight from Montrose on 23rd March 1967, during the last few weeks of steam working along the branch.
C. E. Weston

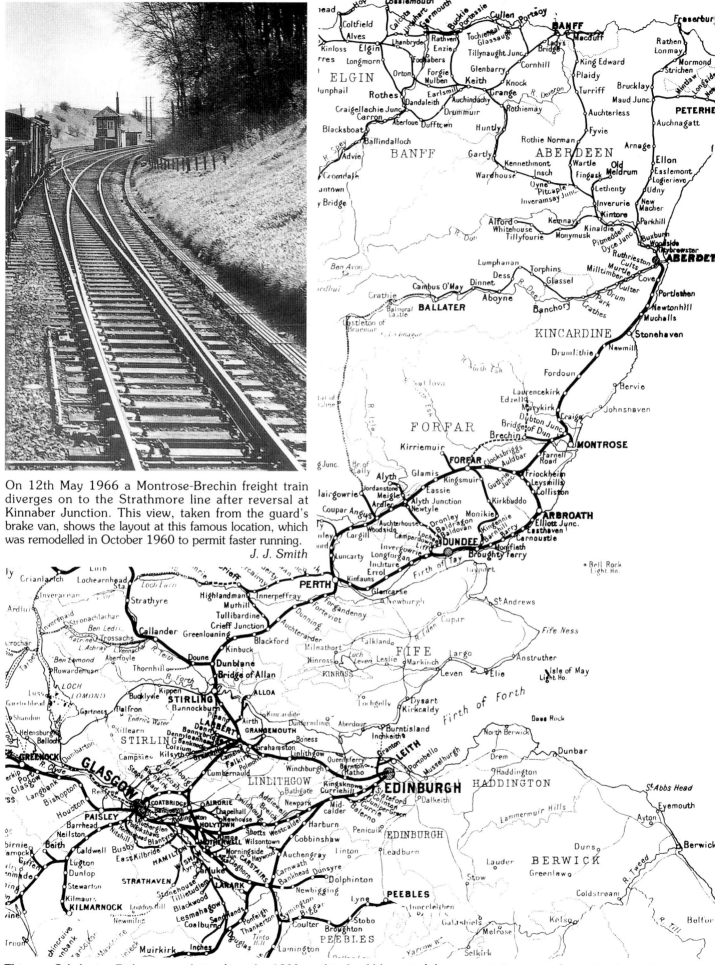

On 12th May 1966 a Montrose-Brechin freight train diverges on to the Strathmore line after reversal at Kinnaber Junction. This view, taken from the guard's brake van, shows the layout at this famous location, which was remodelled in October 1960 to permit faster running.

J. J. Smith

This is a Caledonian Railway map dating from the 1890s and it should be noted that some station names have since been altered.

GLASGOW TO ABERDEEN
THE LAST RACING GROUND OF THE CLASS A4 PACIFICS

by
Tony Davies

'Glasgow to Aberdeen' . . . mention those names to any railway enthusiast who witnessed the painful rundown of steam during the 1960s and his eyes will immediately light up. The line's glittering array of motive power provided an irresistible attraction for the steam-starved enthusiasts of that time. The route was the last refuge of Sir Nigel Gresley's magnificent streamlined Class A4 Pacifics and it is hoped this article will 'set the scene' for the illustrations which follow.

But before I turn to the A4s perhaps a brief history of the pattern of services between the two cities would be appropriate, if only to put the exploits of these locomotives into context with their predecessors. The Glasgow to Aberdeen trunk route links Scotland's principal industrial city with its third largest centre of population. In pre-grouping days rivalry between the Caledonian Railway (CR) and North British Railway (NBR) for the Aberdeen traffic was fierce, the famous races to Aberdeen in 1888 and 1895 being indicative of the keen competition which existed. Generally speaking though, the CR had most of the traffic from Glasgow to Aberdeen, while that from Edinburgh was dominated by the NBR, despite attempts by the CR to poach it with through Aberdeen services from Edinburgh Princes Street. At the turn of the century a traveller from Glasgow using the fastest daytime train could reach Aberdeen in four hours with seven stops, while in the opposite direction a journey time of 3 hr. 55 min. was advertised.

Following the grouping, journey times of under four hours were becoming commonplace as more powerful locomotives became available. In 1924 the 3.25pm from Aberdeen covered the 153 miles to Glasgow in three hours and forty minutes. By 1933 the 10.5am from Glasgow was running to Aberdeen in 3 hr. 30 min. inclusive of eight intermediate stops, a schedule demanding locomotive work of the highest order, with very tight intermediate timings such as eighteen minutes allowed to cover the 16.7 miles between Coupar Angus and Forfar. The advent of the Stanier Class 5s and later the 5XP 'Jubilees' in the latter half of the 1930s ushered in a new era of higher speeds and faster running culminating in the introduction, in the 1937 summer timetable, of two new services timed to run between Glasgow and Aberdeen (and vice versa) in just three hours, albeit with only two stops. This outstanding development was achieved using 'Jubilee' 4-6-0s based at Perth shed, and the trains themselves were named 'The Saint Mungo' and 'The Bon Accord', both of which names were used again in the 1960s.

After the war little attempt appears to have been made to regain pre-war standards of running until June 1956 when a new interval departure timetable was introduced following the closure of twenty-six wayside stations between Glasgow and Aberdeen. Services were accelerated considerably, but still failed to equal the 1937 timings; for example the 12.15pm from Glasgow was speeded-up by 32min. and completed the journey in 3¼ hr. These changes were perhaps disappointing when compared to the June 1962 retimings, but before moving on to these perhaps a reference to LMSR locomotive performance is appropriate at this point. After all, the traditions of the Glasgow to Aberdeen route lay primarily with the LMSR!

The RCTS/SLS 'Aberdeen Flyer' special train travelled north down the East Coast main line on Saturday 2nd June 1962, with A4 Pacific No. 60022, *Mallard,* to Edinburgh and No. 60004, *William Whitelaw,* onwards. The return journey, leaving Aberdeen at 11pm, was worked by 'Princess Royal' Pacifics. No. 46201, *Princess Elizabeth,* worked through the night to Crewe, where No. 46200, *The Princess Royal,* took over for the continuation to London Euston. A real galaxy of main line steam power! Runs with the 'Princess Royal' Pacifics did not often come one's way, and so expectations were at a height at the start of the long overnight run. In the early stages, *Princess Elizabeth* was handled gently. Furthermore, being a Saturday night, the train was sorely delayed by engineering works at Stanley Junction, just north of Perth. So, at 1.30am on a Sunday morning, a good half an hour late away from Perth, and the new crew had a real fight on their hands! These men had no fears in really opening out their engine and the sound effects on the climb to Gleneagles, and then again south of Abington on the main line from Glasgow to Carlisle, were positively awesome. With a 400-ton load, the engine had attained 65mph by Forteviot, just six miles out of Perth, and was then 'going very hard indeed' on the 1 in 121/100 bank up to Gleneagles. The thunder of that 'Princess Royal' in full cry, amongst those Scottish lowland hills, lingered long in the memory! Five minutes were gained to Gleneagles alone and there was more dramatic running on past Larbert – the excitement of timing this great engine at speed was very real! However, there were heavy delays during the long southward run to Euston. The railway historian O. S. Nock has always written with enjoyment of his runs in Scotland and one can read of just what a 5XP 'Jubilee' could do on a train as important as the up 'West Coast Postal', 3.30pm from Aberdeen. This was a lightly loaded and easily timed train, but timekeeping was of great importance. No. 45580, *Burma,* had a load of 299/315 tons – about eight carriages – and was hampered by no less than four separate permanent way slacks between Aberdeen and Forfar alone. Again, the crew of this engine went to it with a will – 83mph at Muchalls (before Stonehaven), 84 at Fordoun and then, by now rather late, a glorious sprint in the high 70s west of Forfar, culminating in 88mph at the River Tay bridge, Cargill, before a fifth permanent way slack. Another recorder had an opportunity of seeing what a 'Princess Royal' could do by way of speed on this train. With a slightly heavier train, No. 46206, *Princess Marie Louise,* had an easy time to Forfar but was then delayed at Eassie, eight miles west of Forfar. Again, they got going and this time a maximum of 88 mph at the River Tay was well sustained onwards to Perth, with a final 82 at Luncarty, four miles out of Perth. That must have been enjoyable!

This just shows a little of the standard of running on this route by the LMSR engines, even down to the mixed-traffic Class 5 4-6-0s, as will be seen later. In 1955, ten years after the end of World War II, the BR Modernisation Plan was published, and was already beginning to have its effect in Scotland by the end of 1960. A three-hour service on the Aberdeen-Edinburgh route had been introduced in April 1960. In July of that year, a DMU service had been started between Aberdeen and Inverness, taking 2½ hours and with two trains each way daily. In December

Gradient Profiles of Glasgow to Aberdeen routes

(courtesy *Railway Magazine*)

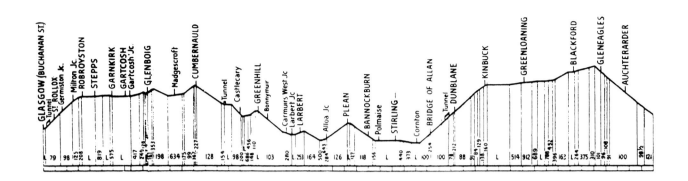

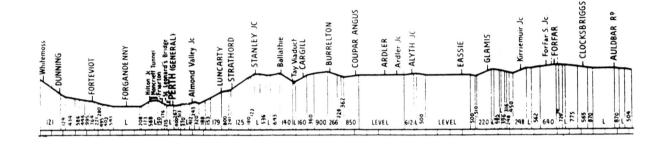

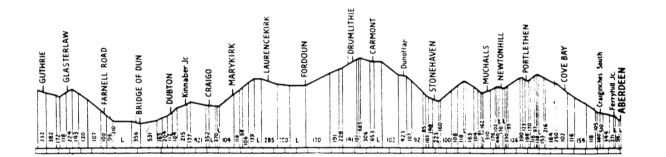

61, English Electric Type 4 diesels – the erstwhile Class 40 which still linger on in preservation – took over the Aberdeen-Edinburgh expresses from Type 2 diesels and steam. By this date the services on the Fort William/Mallaig, Oban and Highland lines north of Perth were virtually all-diesel. So when, against this background, came the first rumours of a three-hour service, using steam power, between Aberdeen and Glasgow it is hard to convey the feelings of incredulity and excitement that such rumours created! If it is hard to convey those feelings amongst the enthusiast fraternity, it is now even harder to convey the atmosphere amongst the men who were to work these trains. To most of the generations who had known only everyday steam, and with the new fast diesels only just starting to make an impact, the thought of Glasgow to Aberdeen in three hours was awe-inspiring. To the enginemen, however, these proposals must have created arguments of far-reaching proportions! G. C. Polyhead, in an article of the time, 'The Big Green Yins', graphically recalls some of the arguments! For the men at the two sheds mainly concerned with these services – Glasgow St. Rollox (Balornock) and Aberdeen Ferryhill – were imbued in a long tradition of LMSR power, interspersed with the newer BR standard designs. And then there were the diesel proponents! 'The Big Green Yins' – what manner of engine could they be? The answer: LNER engines, Classes A3 and A4. One can imagine the consternation among the enginemen at a shed like St. Rollox, where no engines of those types had previously been allocated. And another writer recalls that even at Aberdeen Ferryhill, until the late 1950s, there had been separate LMSR and LNER links; after the merger of links was made each group of men developed a healthy respect for the other's machines! Amid the arguments surrounding the ever-increasing pace of modernisation at that time, there were two important factors that swayed the balance in favour of steam for these trains. The diesels then available in Scotland were of relatively low power, and none too reliable. The NBL D61xx series of 1000/1100 h.p. Type 2 diesel-electrics were particularly notorious for failures, even to the extent of total destruction by fire when out on the road. For a period, this class could not even be trusted to operate passenger trains singly, and so were frequently operated in multiple. Nevertheless, as this account shows, they were persevered with, to the extent that they regularly worked the three-hour trains. On the other hand, in the summer of 1961, the Kings Cross-Edinburgh non-stop 'Elizabethan' expresses, with their invariable A4 power, had finally come to an end. Together with the advent of the 'Deltic' diesel for the faster expresses, these two factors meant that the East Coast route was beginning to have a surplus of low-mileage Pacifics still capable of first-class main line work. Hence it was perhaps inevitable that these much-respected steam engines should find their way on to a route where their power could be used with dramatic effect.

So the equations matched, and A4 No. 60031, *Golden Plover,* was transferred from Haymarket shed, Edinburgh, to Glasgow St. Rollox in order to run a three-hour trial to Aberdeen. This particular A4 had a high mileage, after working the 'Elizabethan' during the 1961 summer, and had the misfortune to drop its middle big end, a common failing of the class. So A4 No. 60027, *Merlin,* recently ex-works from Doncaster, was substituted; it was a curious coincidence that, operating as they did from Haymarket for all of their lives until that time, both of these engines had also had a particular reputation for long periods of continuous operation of the 'Elizabethan'. The trial run took place on 22nd February 1962 and was completely satisfactory, with net times of 164min. and 155min. to/from Aberdeen on an eight-coach load, stopping at Stirling, Perth, Forfar and Stonehaven.

Following the trial run, a reshuffle of motive power took place as a result of which three Haymarket Class A4s – Nos. 60004, *William Whitelaw, 60009, Union of South Africa,* and 60011, *Empire of India* – were transferred to Aberdeen Ferryhill. In addition No. 60027, *Merlin,* was moved to St. Rollox to join its sister locomotive No. 60031. Two Class A3s – Nos. 60090, *Grand Parade,* and 60094, *Colorado,* were also transferred to

St. Rollox to supplement the A4s on the three-hour trains.
So from 18th June 1962, the new service began:

Down (northbound) from Glasgow Buchanan Street
8.25am 'The Grampian'
– the former 8.15 a.m. accelerated by 25min.

5.30pm 'The St. Mungo'
– the former 5.30 p.m. accelerated by 32min.

Up (southbound) from Aberdeen
7.10am 'The Bon Accord'
– the former 6.20 a.m. accelerated by 60min.

5.15pm 'The Granite City'
– the former 6.5pm accelerated by 34min.

Aberdeen Ferryhill shed was of course responsible for the three-hour up morning turn, the engine coming back on the 5.30pm down, while Glasgow St. Rollox worked the down turn in the morning; this returned on the 5.15pm up from Aberdeen. A new 5.30pm up train was also provided to cover the intermediate stops originally made by the 6.5pm. To whet the appetite even more, loads were to be limited to seven carriages, around 250-270 tons, and there were also 60mph start-to-stop bookings between Perth and Forfar. These accelerations were in line with other accelerations on the Highland lines and elsewhere; the overall speed limit throughout Scotland at that time was 75mph. The booked stops conveniently partitioned the line into five distinct sections, each with its own individual character according to the direction of travel. Crews were changed at Perth in both directions, and water was usually taken here also. It is again with a sense of amazement to recall that a reason for the earlier dieselisation of the Edinburgh-Aberdeen route, as a priority, was the difficulty of taking water intermediately at Dundee. The water supply there had always been slow and unreliable, and it had been normal practice for the steam engines, even on the crack London expresses, to be changed as a result. The Aberdeen-Glasgow three-hour trains had to be superimposed on quite a wide variety of other traffic flows, particularly in the Stirling-Perth area. There were the trains from Glasgow to Callander and Oban (on the same route as far as Dunblane), trains coming in from the south at Glenboig, from Edinburgh at Larbert and then the Edinburgh-Inverness direct service at Perth. And, particularly in the 'Scottish Lowland' area, the volume of freight traffic thirty years ago was also far greater than in the 1990s.

Shortly after the revised service began, it became clear that – like most railway operations – it was not going to run quite as smoothly as planned. Within a few weeks of the start of the new timetable both of the St. Rollox A3s had failed at Aberdeen with overheated middle big ends. This prompted the unkind suggestion that the St. Rollox shed staff may have been unaware of the fact that the LNER engines had three, rather than two, cylinders! Another failure during July 1962 was that of A4 No. 60009, which succumbed at Farnell Road, east of Forfar, with similar problems. This temporary shortage of the newly-arrived LNER Pacifics resulted in appearances by Class A2 Pacifics and Class 5 4-6-0s. An unfortunate incident occurred on 6th September 1962 when A3 No. 60094 suffered a brake failure at Buchanan Street and collided with Class 5 No. 45161. The A3 sustained considerable damage to its tender and the Class 5 was subsequently withdrawn. During the same month A4 No. 60004 returned to its former shed at Haymarket, where it remained until June 1963. In November 1962 A4 No. 60012, *Commonwealth of Australia*, was on loan from Edinburgh St. Margarets shed to St. Rollox to cover for two failures by No. 60031. Variations on the motive power in use on the three-hour trains continued to be noted and even Class V2 2-6-2s could be seen in action from time to time. One such occasion was in early December 1962 when No. 60919 – an old stalwart of Ferryhill for many years – worked on the Aberdeen three-hour turn a couple of times. Another noteworthy event, during the first half of 1963, was the transfer of A3 No. 60042, *Singapore,* to Aberdeen Ferryhill, the first of its class to be shedded there in the post-war years. Interlopers continued to be recorded on the three-hour trains at various times and even the appearance of a Class A1 Pacific was not unknown. Among those recorded were No. 60161, *North British,* No. 60162, *Saint Johnstoun,* both from Edinburgh Haymarket, and even a locomotive from Doncaster shed, No. 60157, *Great Eastern!* On 29th June 1963, one of Ferryhill's A2s, No. 60527, *Sun Chariot,* worked the 8.25am down. Its appearance was probably explained by the absence of A4s Nos. 60027/31 at Doncaster works at this time. On 10th July 1963, Class 5 No. 44923 was reported as 'having done magnificently' on the 5.15pm from Aberdeen; again, on 15th August another Class 5, No. 44794, was on the St. Rollox three-hour turn, in both directions. The running of the Stanier Class 5 4-6-0s on these turns proved to be in no way inferior to the bigger LNER engines, and any loss of time could usually be put down to taking water at Perth. A4 No. 60031 was back in action, on the St. Rollox three-hour turn, by mid-August 1963. So matters went on, day in, day out, with the LNER Pacifics gradually winning acceptance among the men. Indeed, writers of the time frequently commented on how the enginemen, from whatever local shed, took so readily to the A3s and A4s. While the firemen soon became familiar with the techniques of firing the LNER Pacifics, it was also commented that the St. Rollox men seemed to treat them sometimes like LMSR engines, i.e. with boilers and fireboxes full, resulting in burnt-out superheater elements on occasions. Certainly, the latter comment was heard in late 1962, and a feature that was noticed on my own runs behind the St. Rollox A3s in 1963 was the continual blowing-off when out on the open road. To add to all the controversies, other writers were quick to comment on how the then-new Type 2 diesels were quite capable of equalling the work of the steam engines.

In early August 1963, a diesel made a first appearance on the three-hour trains, on the 8.25am down and 5.15pm up. This was North British/GEC Type 2 diesel electric No. D6123, which in early March 1963 had been sent to Colchester to have its NBL/MAN diesel engine replaced by a Paxman Ventura engine (1350h.p.). Although 'Standard' NBL diesels did appear from time to time, there seemed to be a preference for using No. D6123 on this duty. An incidental advantage was that a diesel could also be used for a return trip to Fraserburgh – still then open for passenger service – during the layover at Aberdeen. In September 1963 the diesels, No. D6123 and also the occasional Type 2 of the Birmingham RC&W/Sulzer variety, began to appear with greater regularity. No. D6123 itself worked a three-hour trial run, via Dundee, in that month. So, even then, eventual closure of the Strathmore route was contemplated. Thus it seemed, that after only a year or so, the writing was 'on the wall' for steam on the three-hour services – and most enthusiasts were glad to at least have had a run or two with steam in 1963. However, diesel availability became so bad by the middle of 1964 that steam continued, with all its variety, until its final demise in the autumn of 1966. Despite this, and as if to add to the general uncertainty for the enthusiast – even in those years there was not the same vast amount of information that there is today – there was a tendency for the occasional period of regular diesel operation to occur.

A total of nine Class A4s were transferred from English sheds to the Scottish Region in October 1963, but only two of these, Nos. 60005, *Sir Charles Newton,* and 60010, *Dominion of Canada,* went straight into traffic, at Ferryhill. The remainder were put into store at various locations as detailed in the table. Two Haymarket-based locomotives, Nos. 60012, *Commonwealth of Australia,* and 60024, *Kingfisher,* were also put into store at about this time, both being despatched to Dalry Road shed. The latter engine was not, apparently, completely idle during its sojourn there as it was reported in use on various

passenger workings from Edinburgh Princes Street station such destinations as Stirling, Carstairs and Carlisle! Duri October 1963 one of St. Rollox shed's Class A3 Pacifi No.60090, *Grand Parade,* was withdrawn from service, leavi No. 60094, *Colorado,* as the sole representative of its class the former LMSR shed.

The most active Class A4s at Ferryhill during the late autun of 1963 were Nos. 60004/5/10/11/2 with No. 60010, recent recruit from the former GN main line, being a fai consistent performer on the 7.10am Aberdeen-Glasgow a 5.30pm return. During a large part of the summer and autun No. 60009 was at Doncaster. It was away from its home sh for almost four months receiving a general repair, which prov to be the last scheduled overhaul to a steam locomotive at th famous works. Perhaps the most interesting working on t Glasgow to Aberdeen line at this time was the 1.30pm e Aberdeen, the locomotive of which generally returned to Ferryh on an overnight passenger turn from Glasgow. These train nominally rostered for a Class V2 2-6-2, were some of the l regular V2 workings in the country at this time but A3s al appeared, No. 60052, *Prince Palatine,* being noted on 30 November, while in January 1964 V2s recorded on this tra included Nos. 60813/24/35/6.

In February the last remaining Class A3 at St. Rollox, N 60094, *Colorado,* was withdrawn, and the following mon Ferryhill lost one of its stud of A4s when No. 60005, *S Charles Newton,* sustained a cracked cylinder and gained t dubious distinction of becoming the first of Ferryhill's allocati to be condemned. No. 60016, *Silver King,* previously Gateshead engine and latterly stored at Kittybrewster, replac No. 60005, being noted on the 5.30pm from Glasgow on 16 March. During April the 8.25am Buchanan Street to Aberde and 5.15pm back were rostered for diesel traction for the fi time in the form of No. D6123, the re-engined NBL Type 2. May another Ferryhill Class A4, No. 60011, *Empire of Ind* which had worked the first up three-hour train in June 196 was withdrawn at Darlington works following damage sustain in a collision with the buffer stops at Buchanan Street in Marc This loss was more than compensated for by the emergen from store of some of the former 'English' locomotives, N 60006/23/6/34 all being moved up to Aberdeen during t spring of 1964. The only member of the class still inactive w No. 60007, *Sir Nigel Gresley,* which was presumably still store at Dalry Road shed: it was released from storage in Ju During the autumn of 1964 the A4s were in demand for r tours. On 26th September, Nos. 60007 and 60009 worked t RCTS 'Scottish Lowlander' tour over various stages. This tr involved A4-haulage over the erstwhile Carlisle to Edinbur Waverley route during which No. 60007 put up one of the fin A4 performances ever recorded. Later, on 24th October N 60009 became the last A4 to visit Kings Cross when it power the RCTS/SLS 'Jubilee Requiem' tour. After this exertion worked back to Scotland 'light engine' and eventually appeared the head of the 5.30pm from Buchanan Street six days later.

It was perhaps during the last months of 1964 when the hi point of A4 activity was reached, Ferryhill shed alone having total of ten locomotives on its books. In addition a further tw machines, Nos. 60027/31, were based at St. Rollox for use the 8.25am from Glasgow to Aberdeen and 5.15pm retu when a diesel locomotive was unavailable, and these engines al had regular work on the Glasgow to Dundee trains. September 1964 St. Rollox shed lost one of its two A4s wh No. 60027 was transferred to St. Margarets shed, Edinburg where it joined No. 60024. There the pair found employme on various duties, including freight turns to Carlisle, via t Waverley route, Newcastle and Aberdeen. The large number operational A4s at this time meant that Ferryhill shed cou sometimes look like Kings Cross Top Shed a few yea previously: on 12th November seven A4s were noted, includi Nos. 60012/23, both then recently withdrawn. On New Yea Eve, four A4s were seen at Stirling on express passenger work under three hours, in addition to thirteen other steam workings

This classic photograph, which depicts Class A4 No. 60009, *Union of South Africa,* leaving Stonehaven with the 7.10am from Aberdeen on 20th March 1965, has been published on at least two previous occasions. It is, however, one of the author's all-time personal favourite railway photographs which (in his view!) more than justifies its inclusion in this album.

C. E. Weston

The diagrams for the Ferryhill Class A4s during the 1965 summer timetable are set out below:

1.	7.10am	Aberdeen – Glasgow
	5.30pm	Glasgow – Aberdeen
2.	1.30pm	Glasgow – Aberdeen
	11.02pm	Glasgow – Aberdeen SX
	11.02pm	Glasgow – Perth SO
	12.55am	Perth – Aberdeen MO
3.	5.30pm	Aberdeen – Perth SX
	6.44pm	Aberdeen – Perth SO
	6.30am	Perth – Aberdeen

4.	9.10am	Aberdeen – Edinburgh SO
	6.30pm	Millerhill – Aberdeen SO (freight)
		(26th June until 21st August)
5.	7.45pm	Aberdeen – Edinburgh FO
	10.30am	Edinburgh – Aberdeen SO
		(25th June until 28th August)

During the first half of 1965 A4s continued to be a familiar sight on the Aberdeen road and by this time the 1.30pm from there to Glasgow and 11.2pm return train were also a regular job for the class. In March No. 60016, *Silver King,* was taken out of service and in late April was seen dumped at the back of Perth shed minus its nameplates. Two months later No. 60010, *Dominion of Canada,* became the next casualty when it was withdrawn during a visit to Darlington works, but was later purchased for preservation in Canada. At about this time Nos. 60019, *Bittern,* and 60034, *Lord Faringdon,* resumed activity at Ferryhill following heavy intermediate repairs at Darlington which included a full repaint.

The enthusiasm of many of the enginemen working on the Glasgow to Aberdeen route at this time was quite remarkable. On 22nd May 1965, No. 60019, *Bittern,* hauling the 5.30pm from Buchanan Street, 'The Saint Mungo', formed of seven coaches, left Perth seven minutes late following a prolonged water stop. Departure from Forfar was still four minutes late, but progress from there was rapid. Kinnaber Junction was passed in 18$^{1}/_{2}$ minutes, Laurencekirk in 25$^{1}/_{4}$ and the Stonehaven arrival was three minutes early! After a one minute stop, departure was two minutes early and Aberdeen was reached at 8.25pm, five minutes early. The driver was truly enthusiastic and the slightest suggestion of a signal check was greeted with long chimes on the whistle. His enthusiasm did not abate with the arrival: pausing in Aberdeen station only long enough to say that 'A4s were a sight better than any diesel any day', he uncoupled, ran around his train and had disappeared in seventy-five seconds! On 7th June No. 60007, *Sir Nigel Gresley,* had an overall gain of ten minutes from Perth to Aberdeen while working the 5.30pm ex-Glasgow. No. 60024, *Kingfisher,* visited Darlington works in June for a 'casual light' repair followed by No. 60004, *William Whitelaw,* in July for similar attention. During the same month the 8.25am Buchanan Street to Aberdeen and 5.15pm return temporarily reverted to steam operation, usually headed by a St. Rollox Standard Class 5, although No. 60031, *Golden Plover,* appeared on at least one occasion.

During the late summer of 1965, A4s were thin on the ground due to various casualties. No. 60006, *Sir Ralph Wedgwood,* was out of action from mid-August at Ferryhill and later withdrawn. In addition No. 60004 was away at Darlington until early September, while No. 60019 spent a long time under repair at Perth. No. 60031 again appeared on the 8.25am from Buchanan Street on August 25th/26th but failed at Perth on the same train the following day. It later returned to service, but was withdrawn in October. The withdrawal of No. 60031 coincided with the appearance of more reconditioned NBL Type 2 diesels which gradually ousted steam from the Dundee trains and were powering the 8.25am Glasgow to Aberdeen and 5.15pm back with increasing regularity. The A4s, however, continued to monopolise the 7.10am from Aberdeen, 'The Bon Accord', and 5.30pm return from Glasgow, 'The Saint Mungo'. During October No. 60019 was the regular locomotive on these trains. The 1.30pm from Aberdeen to Glasgow and 11.2pm back were also still firmly in the hands of A4s, Nos. 60009/24/6/34 being noted during that month. An unusual incident befell No. 60004 whilst working the 5.30pm from Glasgow on 19th November. When the enginemen tried to water their locomotive on arrival at Perth it was discovered that all the water columns in the station area were dry and the engine was despatched to the shed to take water.

1965 ended on a sad note with the withdrawal of No. 60026, *Miles Beevor,* a former stalwart of Kings Cross Top Shed, on 21st December, leaving just six operational A4s.

The new year began badly for the class with the long-expected dieselisation of the 7.10am from Aberdeen and 5.30pm ex-Glasgow taking place from 5th January, using NBL Type 2 locomotives. These ill-fated machines were soon in trouble, however, and on 24th January, seemingly against all the odds, the A4s were back in command! No. 60034 was regular motive power for the 1.30pm from Aberdeen during this month. On 7th February diesels were again tried on the morning train from Aberdeen, but the afternoon working remained steam

worked. During February No. 60007 was withdrawn fro service for preservation, thus reducing the ranks of the A4s s further. In early April Nos. 60004/9 were also out of traffic, t former being cannibalized for spares in order to keep No. 6000 going a little longer. No. 60019's future also appeared to be the balance at this time when a crack appeared in its left-har side frame just ahead of the cylinder. The locomotive wa despatched to Cowlairs works on 4th April to emerge two da later ready for action, with its front numberplate at first invert to read '61009'! Then came the surprise news that the A4 were to be restored to the 8.25am Glasgow – Aberdeen an 5.15pm return for the duration of the summer timetable, startir on 18th April. For the first six weeks No.60019 was regular rostered for these trains much to the delight of many enthusias who patronised them. When *Bittern* was unavailable, a Class generally deputised. Unfortunately, the withdrawal of N 60009 in June left the A4s very thin on the ground, and in Ju the inevitable happened – all three survivors were stopped f repairs simultaneously. *Bittern* spent most of July under repa at Ferryhill shed, while No. 60034 failed at St. Rollox on 5 July and subsequently spent a period in Eastfield repair sho No. 60024 also failed and it, too, retired to Eastfield fc attention. This situation naturally caused great disappointme to many enthusiasts visiting Scotland and many glum expression were to be seen at Buchanan Street and other stations at th sight of NBL Type 2s deputising for the A4s. Class A2 N 60532, *Blue Peter,* was a regular performer on the 1.30p Aberdeen – Glasgow and 11.2pm return during July and th provided some compensation for the dearth of A4s. All th surviving trio eventually resurfaced, but No. 60034 wa withdrawn in August, leaving Nos. 60019/24 to soldier on the end. No. 60024 worked the 1.30pm from Aberdeen on least one occasion during the last week of August, while N 60019 powered the 7.10am Aberdeen/5.30pm Glasgow o 30th/31st August. On 2nd September *Bittern* hauled commemorative special, organised at short notice by the Scotti Region, from Buchanan Street to Aberdeen and return to ma the official end of the class. In the event, however, No. 6002 continued, somewhat spasmodically, in service on freight wo and on 13th September had a final fling on the 5.15p Aberdeen – Glasgow following a diesel failure and returned th following day at the head of the 8.25am from Buchanan Stree thus ensuring the class went out in a blaze of glory.

Against this background, it is fascinating to turn to the real of performance – nothing quite like getting out on the lin taking one's chance and going to see for oneself how the engine were performing on the road. Part of the interest surroundir the three-hour trains was that theoretically time had to be ke without exceeding the 75mph limit then in existence througho the Scottish Region. Not surprisingly, this was not alwa heeded, particularly when late running occurred . . . Indeed, or of the fastest runs on record involves a BR Caprotti Class running at just under 90mph between Perth and Forfar. Th route always had a reputation for hard and resolute running wi steam and one's enthusiasm was whetted, not only by the LNE engines but also by the everyday Class 5s on the slower Glasgo Aberdeen semi-fasts. The *Railway Magazine* for May 196 carries an account of a brilliant piece of time regaining by N 45179, on an eight-carriage train forming the 12.15pm fro Buchanan Street. The Class 5 had taken over from a failure Perth, and left 18 min. late; 8min. were regained to Aberdee Then there was another run with a Class 5 (*Railway Magazin* March 1964) the running of which was described in such term as 'positive savagery' by O.S. Nock! This run, on the 10.15a from Buchanan Street on 8th May 1963, and recorded by R.N Clements, has been well documented elsewhere.

However, there was nothing quite like timing any of the b LNER Pacifics – or LMSR Pacifics if the chance arose! – whe the crew were really in a hurry. This could be an enervatin experience indeed, and, on the occasions when this did happer one could sit back at the end of the run with a sense o satisfaction at having recorded a journey of quality. In the earl

The 10.10 am Aberdeen to Euston, with Class 5 No. 44703 in charge, passes Craiginches on its way out of Aberdeen on 13th July 1965. This train was routed via the Strathmore line and would have more coaches attached at Perth. *S. C. Nash*

960s, journeys by train were still carried out with a sense of xploration and adventure. With all the variety of those days, avel in all its forms had not yet become the rather soul-stroying chore that it seems, perhaps, in the 1990s. Speed in elf has become an even more meaningless parameter when set ainst the ultra-high speed lines of the modern age – even over summit like Druimuachdar, on the Perth-Inverness main line, e line speed, today, is 80mph! The gradient profile provides a ide to the 'ups and downs' of the Aberdeen route through rfar; what is not so easy to envisage are the number of minor acks which tended to interrupt any prolonged high-speed forts. The severe speed restriction through Larbert was a case point, and again in the down direction at Kinnaber Junction. amples of other slacks that come to mind were the curves, sociated with the railway history of the area, at Guthrie and at

Farnell Road, between Forfar and Bridge of Dun. To the recording enthusiast the Glasgow to Aberdeen line carried a special aura of appeal during the drab years of the 1960s when the onward spread of dieselisation seemed unstoppable. Small groups of enthusiasts would congregate at platform ends, at certain times of the day, and exchange notes before dashing off for yet another hectic run behind a Pacific, Class 5 or whatever. The tremendous atmosphere of enthusiasm was also apparent amongst the crews – sometimes it seemed as though that melodious A4 chime whistle was on the go all the way from Glasgow to Aberdeen ......! With one exception I have drawn upon my own personal experiences to illustrate some of the running on the Glasgow-Aberdeen three-hour trains. What I have written is not meant to prove anything, is not necessarily of a record-breaking nature but just a record of chance happenings.

Hopefully they bring to life the unexpected and the excitement, of recording mainline steam in action amidst the everyday process of operating the railway. As always, speed is relative to the ground conditions, uphill or downhill, curves and the state of the track, and, above all, the degree of effort expended by the engine crew on that sometimes difficult beast, the steam locomotive. In running their trains to time, the ingenuity of the engine crews could sometimes be taxed to the limit!

My first run on this route with an A4 was on the grey, cloudy evening of 12th July 1963. No.60011, *Empire of India,* on the 5.30pm down, was already up against it by Stirling. Nearly nine minutes late away from here, an eight-carriage load and two p.w. slacks meant that nothing could be gained to Perth. Then, on to Forfar, all the symptoms of trouble on the footplate were apparent, with the engine eased back at Burrelton and making only 65mph or so passed Alyth Junction. The train was sixteen minutes down at Forfar! While taking water here, the crew were able to bring things round on the footplate sufficiently in order to have a bit of a go at the next stage on to Stonehaven. So, setting off into the gathering dusk of a summer's evening, and behind an engine obviously not in good shape, there was all the excitement of a hard and fast run in the making. With the exhaust beat from the engine more or less a continuous roar, there was a dramatic acceleration from Forfar to 80mph after Auldbar Road, and taking the curve at Guthrie with an even more vicious bump than usual in the process. Like so many brief glimpses of great efforts with steam, mere words and figures cannot capture the dash and fire of the moment . . . through Glasterlaw in just over nine minutes, the engine was eased down Farnell Road bank. Then, in attempting to force the pace again, on the level stretch towards Bridge of Dun, No.60011 slipped. In these circumstances, there was then nothing for it but for the crew to now take matters easily, on through the lonely Mearns country to Stonehaven, with 50mph at the summit beyond

Marykirk and only 61mph past Fordoun. Still fourteen minut late, another furious start was made from Stonehaven. Th summit at MP 227½, after two miles of 1 in 100/118 up an with the engine working on full regulator and 50% cut-off, w cleared in 4½ min at 42mph and then came 71mph Muchalls and 60mph at Portlethen, followed by a perfectly cle road, taken with great swiftness, right into Aberdeen. This fir lap took just under nineteen minutes, so finishing ten minut late. Hard now to remember the excitement of those speedi moments!

The following morning I returned to Perth on the 7.10a up, behind No.60004, *William Whitelaw,* on a seven-carria load. On a rail wet with morning dew, causing the engine slip on starting, this run was a model of decorum, with easin for the state of the track where necessary. Forfar was left 2 minutes late, still slipping in getting away, but the crew then p up a remarkably even run, at a steady 80mph all the way fro Glamis to Coupar Angus (eleven miles) followed by 73mph Burrelton and 83 at the River Tay. This was a glorious run the early morning sunshine – on time at Perth, in just ov twenty-nine minutes from Forfar.

Exactly a year later, in July 1964, while en route to the f north of Scotland, I managed another run on the 5.30pm dov as from Perth, returning on the 7.10am up a few days late This time No. 60010, *Dominion of Canada*, turned up on th down train, with the normal seven-carriage load. Again, eve though time was kept, matters seemed rather suspect on th stretch to Forfar. A gentle start was made from here, and th engine not opened out until Bridge of Dun. Then we ha another half-hour of thrilling running, with the A4 going in gre style, 61mph at Marykirk and all of 75mph past Fordoun 'Thank God they're past', as the stationmaster used to say to th signalman in the days of the North British Atlantics! A go start was made from Stonehaven, clearing the MP 227 summit at 45mph, but the rest of the run was taken quietl Aberdeen was reached six minutes late after being nearly twel minutes late away from Forfar. Coming back on the 7.10am u this time we had the immortal No. 60009, which demonstrat just what a really good A4 could do with the normal seven-coa load. This time I went on to Stirling, and the time from Per was just over thirty-five minutes; another report shows what th engine could do when really pressed – four minutes faster, wi 79mph at Dunning, 56½ mph at Gleneagles and 85 Greenloaning! Really moving here!

As things turned out, the A4s soldiered on until the end, September 1966. It is pleasing to be able to refer to a log of run recorded by S.C. Nash in July 1966, during the closin weeks of steam. No. 60024, *Kingfisher,* was on the dov morning train and with only a six-carriage load, 215/230 tor Perth to Forfar was run in twenty-nine minutes (thirty-o schedule), with a steady 80-plus after Coupar Angus and maximum of 85 at Kirriemuir Junction, three miles from th stop. Then there was 70mph at Guthrie, Glasterlaw passed 10½ minutes and 77mph down Farnell Road bank. Th impetus meant that the undulating road on to Marykirk ar Stonehaven could be carried in much the same manner as on n own run with *Dominion of Canada;* this stretch was run 39½ minutes (43 schedule). Then came a fast run in Aberdeen, in just over eighteen minutes, with 70mph in the di at Muchalls, Portlethen and on the final descent. As th passengers alighted from the train, there must have been a fe wistful backward glances, in the realisation that this could rea be one of the last runs in normal service. It must have been happy sense of coincidence that *Kingfisher* should figure largely in the last days – unforgettable journeys with stear Connoisseurs of A4 performance would remember that the san engine, *Kingfisher,* was responsible for one tremendous wartin feat that has been well chronicled: Newcastle to Edinburgh with 610-ton load, touching 83mph near Beal, south of Berwick. It fortunate that we have so many photographs of the A4s out the road that convey the sense of power and majesty of the cla at speed .....

8.15am Forfar to Perth

Saturday 13th July 1963

A4 60004 *William Whitelaw*

7 carriages, 256 tons tare, 270 tons gross

Miles		min.	sec.	Speed
0.0	Forfar dep.	0	00	
0.7	Forfar South Junction	1	52	38
2.9	Kirriemuir Junction	4	07	48/65
5.7	Glamis	6	26	71/74
7.9	Eassie	8	05	79/80
12.0	Alyth Junction	11	08	80
14.2	Ardler	12	50	80
16.7	Coupar Angus	14	39	80
18.9	Burrelton	16	25	78/73
21.2	Cargill	18	17	74/76
23.1	Ballathie S.B.	19	38	83
25.3	Stanley Junction	21	25	76
27.4	Strathord	22	59	76
30.9	Almond Valley Junction	25	57	74
32.5	Perth arr.	29	15	

9.45am Perth to Forfar

Wednesday 13th July 1966

A4 60024 *Kingfisher*

6 carriages, 215 tons tare, 230 tons gross

(Recorded by S.C. Nash)

Miles		min.	sec.	Speed
0.0	Perth dep.	0	00	
4.2	Luncarty	6	11	59
7.2	Stanley Junction	9	05	62/58
11.3	Cargill	12	36	76
13.6	Burrelton	14	25	72/80
15.8	Coupar Angus	16	08	76
18.3	Ardler	18	02	80
20.5	Alyth Junction	19	45	81
24.6	Eassie	22	46	83
26.8	Glamis	24	21	82
29.6	Kirriemuir Junction	26	21	85
32.5	Forfar arr.	29	06	

Perhaps the final word for steam on the Glasgow-Aberdeen ┊te should lie with the 'West Coast Postal'. My very first run ┊ a three-hour train in fact had been on Monday 13th April ┊63, behind A3 No. 60094, *Colorado,* on the 8.25am down. ┊is was a very good run with an engine easily master of its job, ┊iving in Aberdeen 3½ minutes early. For a first run this ┊ckly showed the magic of a run behind steam on this route .... ┊at day I returned south on the up 'Postal', at 3.30pm from ┊erdeen, worked by Ferryhill's newly acquired A3 No. 60042, ┊*gapore*. Booked to Perth in 97 minutes, with one stop for ┊ter at Forfar, this was a memorable run on a pleasant day of ┊ly spring sunshine, with an engine once again master of the ┊. At Perth, after No. 60042 had departed for Carstairs with ┊ Royal Mail vans, Class 5 4-6-0 No. 44961 took over for the ┊ntinuation to Glasgow; a three-coach Perth-Edinburgh portion ┊s detached at Larbert to be worked forward from there by a ┊ Standard 2-6-4T, No. 80060. Just a glimpse of the ┊ormous variety in the trains to be found on Scottish Region ┊tals in those days. In July 1963 I enjoyed a similar down run ┊ the 8.25am with No. 60100 *Spearmint*.

The end of the Class A4s did not mean the complete ┊mination of steam traction from the route and isolated ┊pearances continued to be reported. On 5th October 1966 ┊ass V2 No. 60836 took over the 4.0pm Edinburgh to ┊erdeen following a diesel failure at Dundee, while A2 Pacific ┊. 60532, *Blue Peter* was still active there. On 29th October ┊owered the 7.20pm freight to Craiginches. A special train to ┊nmemorate the end of V2s was organised by Scottish Region, ┊ng No. 60836. This train ran on 5th November from ┊inburgh to Aberdeen and back. Another sad event during the ┊ne weekend was the closure of Glasgow Buchanan Street ┊tion which had been the starting point for so many ┊morable journeys during the last few years of steam. During ┊vember the last regular steam turn on the Glasgow to ┊erdeen route, the 7.0pm Perth to Aberdeen stopping train ┊nt over to Type 2 diesel haulage.

Occasional passenger workings were even noted in 1967,

such as the appearance of 'Britannia' Pacific No. 70041, *Sir John Moore,* on the 7.15am local passenger from Perth to Aberdeen on 16th February, but by this time such workings were exceptional. A pocket of steam, consisting largely of Class B1 4-6-0s and J37 0-6-0s, was still active from Dundee Tay Bridge shed on freight work and remained so until the end of April, when steam officially became a thing of the past on Scottish Region. Prior to this, on 25th March, A4 No. 60009, *Union of South Africa,* piloted by Class 5 No. 44997, hauled the ScR's 'Grand Easter Tour' from Perth to Aberdeen via the Strathmore route. The massive eighteen coach train of 602 tons tare was whisked along the 89.8 miles between the two cities in 87 min. .... a spectacular performance, without doubt! The same machines later returned the excursionists from Perth to Edinburgh, from where No. 60009 proceeded to Thornton Junction shed prior to moving to its new home at the Lochty Railway, Fife. On 20th May sister locomotive No. 4498, *Sir Nigel Gresley,* another former resident of Ferryhill, traversed the Perth-Forfar-Aberdeen route during a railtour from Glasgow which returned from Aberdeen via Dundee. This was the last recorded steam working along the Strathmore route prior to its closure four months later.

In 1987 I had a rare opportunity of returning from Aberdeen southwards by train, obviously via Dundee, Perth and Stirling – I can remember nothing about it! Apart from the occasional appearance of a preserved engine – and even in 1993 it is good to record that No. 60009 has been active on this road – the A4s have long since passed from the scene. And as for the Strathmore route – 'the line the Grampians rode' – perhaps I can quote A.G. Dunbar writing in the *Journal of the Stephenson Locomotive Society* (October 1967) '.... now the Strathmore route has been closed and a chapter of Scottish history has been ended – not without regret on the part of many ...... my last steam run was behind *Golden Plover* and a friend with me timed her at over 90 through Cargill.' Thus do we remember them.

Although the LMSR Class 5 4-6-0s proved themselves to be such capable performers, perhaps, with a bit of conjecture, and also allowing for the loyalties at the western end of the line, the big LMSR Pacifics might have been suited to those trains? After all, there were plenty of those superb engines around, and still in good condition, in October 1963! History has had its fling, however, and we treasure great memories of how the LNER Pacifics managed to 'time' the three-hour Glasgow-Aberdeen service with such a high degree of regularity and reliability.

CLASS A4 PACIFICS ACTIVE ON GLASGOW – ABERDEEN ROUTE 1962 – 1966

Loco No.	Name	Former Shed	Stored at	Date Transferred to Aberdeen	Date Withdrawn	Remarks
60004	*William Whitelaw*	64B	–	11.6.62	17.7.66	Returned to 64B 20.9.62 – 17.6.63
60005	*Sir Charles Newton*	52A	–	10.11.63	12.3.64	Based at 64A 28.10.63 – 10.11.63
60006	*Sir Ralph Wedgwood*	34E	Dalry Road	4.5.64	3.9.65	
60007	*Sir Nigel Gresley*	34E	Dalry Road	20.7.64	1.2.66	
60009	*Union of South Africa*	64B	–	20.5.62	1.6.66	
60010	*Dominion of Canada*	34E	–	20.10.63	29.5.65	
60011	*Empire of India*	64B	–	11.6.62	11.5.64	
60012	*Commonwealth of Australia*	64B	Dalry Road	20.1.64	20.8.64	
60016	*Silver King*	52A	Kittybrewster	10.11.63	19.3.65	Taken out of store 3.64
60019	*Bittern*	52A	Kittybrewster	10.11.63	5.9.66	Date removed from store not known
60023	*Golden Eagle*	52A	Bathgate	17.5.64	30.10.64	
60024	*Kingfisher*	64B	Dalry Road	6.5.65	5.9.66	Based at 64A 15.12.63 – 6.5.65
60026	*Miles Beevor*	34E	Bathgate	13.4.64	21.12.65	Stored at Galashiels until 12.63
60027	*Merlin*	64B	–	20.5.62*	3.9.65	Based at 64A from 6.9.64
60031	*Golden Plover*	64B	–	3.2.62*	29.10.65	
60034	*Lord Faringdon*	34E	Bathgate	17.5.64	24.8.66	Stored at Galashiels until 12.63

Key to shed codes:
34E Peterborough (New England): 52A Gateshead: 64A St. Margarets: 64B Haymarket: *St. Rollox, Glasgow

REFERENCES

Locomotives of the LNER Part 2A (R.C.T.S. 1978).
The Gresley Pacifics, O.S.Nock (David & Charles 1982)
Scottish Railways, O.S. Nock (Thomas Nelson 1950)
Stanier 4-6-0s at Work, A.J. Powell (Ian Allan 1983)
Travelling Hopefully, The Gulbenkian Foundation 1992
Locomotive Performance, R.I. Nelson (Ian Allan 1979)
Railway Magazine
Modern Railways
Railway World
Journal of the Stephenson Locomotive Society
The Railway Observer (R.C.T.S.)

Table 32 — GLASGOW (Buchanan Street), EDINBURGH (Princes Street), STIRLING, PERTH, DUNDEE and ABERDEEN

Week Days

Miles from Edinburgh / Miles from Gleneagles

Stations:
- Glasgow (Buch. St.) ... dep
- Coatbridge (Cen.) ... dep
- Cumbernauld
- Greenhill
- Edinburgh (Prin. St.) ... dep
- Falkirk (Grahamston) ... dep
- Larbert ... arr
- Stirling ... dep
- Bridge of Allan
- Dunblane
- Gleneagles
- Tullibardine
- Muthill
- Strageath Halt
- Highlandman
- Pittenzie Halt
- Crieff ... arr
- Comrie ... arr
- Perth (Princes St.) ... arr
- Errol
- Invergowrie
- Dundee (West) ... arr
- Dundee (Tay B'dge) ... arr
- Inverness ... arr
- Coupar Angus
- Alyth Junction
- Forfar
- Bridge of Dun
- Laurencekirk
- Stonehaven
- Aberdeen ... arr

Named trains / connections noted in columns: THE ROYAL HIGHLANDER, THE GRAMPIAN, THE GRANITE CITY, THE BON ACCORD.

For Notes, see page 332

Table 32 — GLASGOW (Buchanan Street), EDINBURGH (Princes Street), STIRLING, PERTH, DUNDEE and ABERDEEN—continued

Week Days

For Notes, see page 332

Table 32— *continued*

GLASGOW (Buchanan Street), EDINBURGH (Princes Street), STIRLING, PERTH, DUNDEE and ABERDEEN

Week Days—continued

	pm D 🅑	pm 1 15	pm E D	pm E S	pm S 1 35		pm E 2 5 2	pm S 5	pm D	pm D 🅑		pm 3 15		pm E 3 41	pm D D	pm D		pm 4 0	pm S
Glasgow (Buch. St.).. dep		1 15			1 35		2 5 2 5			🅑		3 15						4 0	
Coatbridge (Cen.).. dep														3 41					
Cumbernauld																			
Greenhill																			
20 Edinburgh (Prin.St.) dep			1 8	1 8	1 8		2 17 2 17					3 13		3 53				3 53	
20 Falkirk (Grahamston) ,,			1 46	1 48	1 48		2 17 2 17					3 13		3 53				3 53	
Larbert .... arr			1 52	1 54	2 10		2 37 2 37					3 47		4		4 23		4 25	
dep		1 56	1 54	1 55	2 12		2 38 2 38					3 48		4 1		4 36		4 36	
Stirling........... arr		2 0	2 42	5 2	2 23		2 49 2 49					3 59		4 15		4 40		4 40	
dep		2 0	2 42	5 2	2 26		2 52 2 52 3	6				3 59		4 19					
Bridge of Allan ...								3 21											
Dunblane		2 10					3 15 3 15	3 17						4 25	4 25		4 48	5 5	
Gleneagles		2T15						3T22							4 54	4T53				
Tullibardine		2 21					3 27								4 59				
Muthill		2T26						3T31							5T2				
Strageath Halt		2T28						3T33							5T5				
Highlandman		2T30						3T35							5T8				
Pittenzie Halt		2 32					3 37	3 37							5 10				
Crieff ..... { arr																			
{ dep																			
Comrie ..... arr																			
Perth .... arr		2 38		3 7			3 43 3 41	3 35						4 45	5 3		5 33	5 24	
Perth .... dep		2 40		3 13			3 43 3 41							4 17	5 3		5 35	5 34	
Perth (Princes St.)..														4 32			5 59		
Errol														4 41					
Invergowrie																			
Dundee (West).. arr		3 10												4 49			6 6		
Dundee (Tay B'dge) arr																			
35 Inverness .... arr							7 50 7 50								9 25			9 25	
Coupar Angus... dep																			
Alyth Junction			3 39				4 9 4 9							5 35				5 56	
Forfar			3 54				4 9 4 9												
Bridge of Dun							4 25 4 25							5 56				6 18	
Laurencekirk							4 44 4 44							6 18				6 39	
Stonehaven					4 48		5 15	5 32						6 54				7 15	
Aberdeen ... ... arr					5 11		5 40 5 40	5 52						7 17				7 38	

Week Days—continued

	pm S	pm		pm	pm D	pm	pm V		pm D	pm 5 0		pm 5 12	pm S 5 30	pm 5 35			pm 6 5		pm	pm E	pm 6 15	pm D 🅑
Glasgow (Buch. St.).. dep				4 25		40 30				5 0		5 12	5 30	5 35			6 5				6 15	🅑
Coatbridge (Cen.).. dep	4 26																6 17					
Cumbernauld				4 47									5 57									
Greenhill				4 56									6 6									
20 Edinburgh (Prin.St.) dep	3X46			3X46		4C15				5 17			5 32				6 15				6 15	
20 Falkirk (Grahamston) ,,	4 26					4 59				5 17			5 32				6 15				6 15	
Larbert .... arr		4 47					5					5 41	5 44			6 11	6 32				6 40	
dep		4 49					5 8	5 20		5 33		5 42	5 56	5 58	6		6 34				6 46	
Stirling........... arr		5 4					5 16	5 24		5 36		5 46	6		6 8		6 40				6 46	
dep		5 4					5 17	27		5 38		5 49	6 5		6 16		6 46					
Bridge of Allan ...											5 55			6 16							7K 3	
Dunblane										5 43		5 58	6 13		6 37						7 21	7 28 7 30
Gleneagles												6 55									7 21	7 35
Tullibardine												6T10										7 41
Muthill												6T16										7T46
Strageath Halt												6T20										7T48
Highlandman												6T24										7T50
Pittenzie Halt												6 26										
Crieff ..... { arr												6 27										7 52
{ dep												6 29										
Comrie ..... arr												6 39										
Perth .... arr		5 45					6 15			6 5		6 31		6 31			6 46				7 40 7 46	
Perth .... dep										6 22				6 49							7 50	
Perth (Princes St.)..										6 32												
Errol										6 41												
Invergowrie																					8 16	
Dundee (West).. arr										6 48											8 18	
Dundee (Tay B'dge) arr																					8 26	
35 Inverness .... arr				9 25																		
Coupar Angus... dep																						
Alyth Junction																					7 21	
Forfar																7 22					7 29	
Bridge of Dun																					7 45	
Laurencekirk																					8 25	
Stonehaven		7 36														8 7					8 43	
Aberdeen ... ... arr		8 0														8 25					8 46	

For Notes, see page 332

Table 32 *continued*

GLASGOW (Buchanan Street), EDINBURGH (Princes Street), STIRLING, PERTH, DUNDEE, and ABERDEEN

Week Days—continued

	pm 6 22	pm S		pm	pm D 🅑	pm E S	pm 7 30		pm D		pm 8 15		pm	pm	pm E	pm S 1046
Glasgow (Buch. St.).. dep	6 22	6 43			🅑		7 30				8 15		9 15			1046
Coatbridge (Cen.).. dep		6 43											9 15			
Cumbernauld	6 44										8 39		9 37			
Greenhill	6 53										8 48		9 46			
20 Edinburgh (Prin.St.) dep	6 49	6 49					7 50	7 50					9 13		1020	1048
20 Falkirk (Grahamston) ,,	6 49	6 49					8 30	8 30					9 13		1057	1048
Larbert .... arr	6 58	7 4					8 2	8 3		8 36	8 53		9 51		115	117
dep	6 59	7 6					8 3	8 14		8 38	8 55		9 52		115	1120
Stirling........... arr	7 10	7 14					8 14			8 49	9 6		9 6		116	1120
dep	7 13	7 21					8 17				9 10		10 9			1124
Bridge of Allan ...	7 18												9 22			
Dunblane	7 26	7K30					8 33				9 37		9 30			
Gleneagles		7 48					8 33				9 37					
Tullibardine							8T38									
Muthill							8 43									
Strageath Halt							8T48									
Highlandman							8T50									
Pittenzie Halt							8T52									
Crieff ..... { arr							8 54									
{ dep																
Comrie ..... arr																
Perth .... arr		8 10					8 57				9 54					12 5
Perth .... dep							9 3				10 1					
Perth (Princes St.)..											10 18					
Errol							9 22				10 28					
Invergowrie							9 31									
Dundee (West).. arr											10 35					
Dundee (Tay B'dge) arr							9 38				10 35					
35 Inverness .... arr																
Coupar Angus... dep							9 23									
Alyth Junction																
Forfar							9 43									
Bridge of Dun																
Laurencekirk							9 31	9 48	1017							
Stonehaven							9 48	10 5	1035							
Aberdeen ... ... arr							10 10		1025	1056						

Week Days—continued | Sundays

	pm E S	pm E		pm E	pm E S	pm E	am A		am		am	am	am	am	am	am	am D
Glasgow (Buch. St.).. dep	1030			11 0	11 0	1115								7 35			
Coatbridge (Cen.).. dep		11 11												7 35			
Cumbernauld	1054			11 27													
Greenhill	11 3			11 36													
20 Edinburgh (Prin.St.) dep	1020	1035		10 20	1035									8 10			
20 Falkirk (Grahamston) ,,	1057	1114		10 57	11 14									8 10			
Larbert .... arr	11 8	1120		11 31	11 41	1150					5 16			8 10			
dep	1113	1121		11 33	11 54	1152					5 18		8 23	8 12			
Stirling........... arr	1124	1133		11 42	12 4	1230					5 29		8 23	8 27			
dep	1127			11 48	11 59	11 59	12 7				5 34						
Bridge of Allan ...	1134				12a 4												
Dunblane	1139			12 10	12 10		1241							8 36			
Gleneagles					12 29	1232					5 59			8 56			
Tullibardine																	
Muthill																	
Strageath Halt																	
Highlandman																	
Pittenzie Halt																	
Crieff ..... { arr																	
{ dep																	
Comrie ..... arr																	
Perth .... arr				12a31	12a40	12 47	1251				6 18		9 18		259	9 32	9 45
Perth .... dep						12 57	1 25				6 33				259	9 32	9 45
Perth (Princes St.)..																	
Errol																	
Invergowrie																	
Dundee (West).. arr																	
Dundee (Tay B'dge) arr																	10 14
35 Inverness .... arr				5 20		5 20					1055						1255
Coupar Angus... dep																	
Alyth Junction																	
Forfar				1 40									1010				
Bridge of Dun				2 15									1032				
Laurencekirk											6 12		8 23		1024	119	
Stonehaven											6 34		8 48		1047	1135	
Aberdeen ... ... arr				3 20							6 34		8 48		1047	1135	

For Notes, see page 332

Table 32— GLASGOW (Buchanan Street), EDINBURGH (Princes Street), STIRLING, PERTH, DUNDEE and ABERDEEN
continued

Sundays—continued

Stations (left column):
Glasgow (Buchanan St.) dep; Coatbridge (Cen.) dep; Cumbernauld dep; Greenhill; 20 Edinburgh (Prin. St.) dep; 20 Falkirk (Grahamston); Larbert; Stirling; Bridge of Allan; Dunblane; Tullibardine; Gleneagles; Muthill; Strageath Halt; Highlandman; Pitcenzie Halt; Comrie; Crieff; Perth; Perth (Prince St.); Errol; Invergowrie; Inergowrie; Perth; Dundee (Tay B'dge); Dundee (West); Coupar Angus; Alyth Junction; Forfar; Bridge of Dun; Laurencekirk; Stonehaven; Aberdeen.

Notes (legend):
- **A** Except Mondays
- **B** Passengers can arr Dundee 11 43 am by changing at Kirkcaldy
- **C** Dep 4 22 pm on Saturdays
- **D** Diesel Service
- **E** Arr 6 41 am or E Except Saturdays
- **F** Calls Carnoustie until 25th August only
- **H** Arr 3 minutes later until 25th August inclusive
- **J** Stops to set down on advice being given to the guard prior to arrival of the train at Carstairs
- **K** Stops to set down from Carlisle and South thereof on notice at Stirling
- **L** Dep Glasgow (Central) Station
- **M** Mondays only
- **MB** Miniature Buffet Car
- **p** pm
- **P** Dep Glasgow (Queen Street) Station
- **RB** Buffet Car
- **RC** Restaurant Car
- **S** or S Saturdays only
- **SC** Sleeping Car
- **TC** Through Carriages
- **T** Stops if required to set down on notice to the guard or to take up when there are passengers on the platform
- **V** Diesel service except on Saturdays
- **W** Arrives Falkirk (Grahamston)
- **X** Departs from Edinburgh (Waverley)
- **②** Second class only

For LOCAL TRAINS and intermediate Stations between Edinburgh (Wav.) and Falkirk, see Table 20 between Glasgow and Aberdeen, Table 27—Edinburgh and Stirling, Table 27—Edinburgh and Aberdeen, Table 27

For OTHER TRAINS between Glasgow and Aberdeen, Table 27—Edinburgh (Wav.), and Falkirk, see Table 20 and Perth, Table 27—Edinburgh and Aberdeen, Table 27

Within table notes:
- TC Glasgow to Montrose via Dundee (Tay Bridge)
- Arr Carnoustie 12.5 pm, Arbroath 12.11 pm, Montrose 12.35 pm (Table 27)
- RC Glasgow to Aberdeen
- SC and TC Glasgow to Inverness

Table 31— ABERDEEN, DUNDEE, PERTH, STIRLING, EDINBURGH (Princes Street) and GLASGOW (Buchanan Street)
continued

Week Days

Miles column and Stations:
Aberdeen dep; Stonehaven; Laurencekirk; Bridge of Dun; Forfar; Alyth Junction; Coupar Angus; Dundee (Tay B'dge) dep; Dundee (West); Invergowrie; Errol; Perth; Perth (Princes St.); Crieff; Comrie; Perth; Gleneagles; Muthill; Highlandman; Strageath Halt; Dunblane; Tullibardine; Bridge of Allan; Stirling; Larbert; 20 Falkirk (Grahamston) arr; 20 Edinburgh (Prin. St.) arr; Greenhill; Cumbernauld; Coatbridge (Cen.); Glasgow (Buch. St.) arr.

Miles from Larbert column.

Within table notes:
- SC and TC Inverness to Glasgow and Edinburgh (Waverley)
- To Glasgow (Cen.) Low Level arr 7 37 am
- TC Thornton Junction dep 7 3 am (Table 27)
- TC Callander dep 7 52 am to Glasgow (Table 33)
- TC Arbroath dep 6 28 am (Table 27)
- TC Aberdeen to London (King's Cross)
- MB and TC Aberdeen to Edinburgh (Waverley)
- MB Dundee to Glasgow
- TC Dundee to Edinburgh

Stations (lower table, left): Aberdeen dep; Stonehaven; Laurencekirk; Bridge of Dun; Forfar; Alyth Junction; Coupar Angus; Dundee (Tay B'dge) dep; Dundee (West); Invergowrie; Errol; Perth; Perth (Princes St.); Crieff; Comrie; Perth; Gleneagles; Muthill; Highlandman; Strageath Halt; Pitcenzie Halt; Dunblane; Tullibardine; Bridge of Allan; Stirling; Larbert; 20 Falkirk (Grahamston) arr; 20 Edinburgh (Prin. St.); Greenhill; Cumbernauld; Coatbridge (Cen.); Glasgow (Buch. St.) arr.

Week Days

Within table notes:
- THE BON ACCORD. MB Aberdeen to Glasgow except Saturdays
- RB Aberdeen to Glasgow Saturdays only
- TC Oban dep 6 15 am to Glasgow (Table 33)
- TC Aberdeen to London (King's Cross)
- To Edinburgh (Waverley)
- RC, MB and TC Perth to London (Euston) arr 7.22 pm
- TC Arbroath dep 8 8 am (Table 27)
- TC Oban dep 6 15 am to Edinburgh (Table 33)
- TC Dundee to Manchester (Vic.) arr 5 33 pm
- TC Aberdeen to Manchester (Vic.) arr 5 33 pm
- MB Dundee to Glasgow
- Runs 29th June to 31st August inclusive
- TC Aberdeen to Glasgow via Montrose. Dep Montrose 9 46 am, Arbroath 10 7 am (Table 27)
- Runs 29th June to 24th August inclusive
- TC Aberdeen to Edinburgh (Waverley)

For Notes, see page 337

Table 32—continued

ABERDEEN, DUNDEE, PERTH, STIRLING, EDINBURGH (Princes Street) and GLASGOW (Buchanan Street)

Week Days—continued

Station list (common to the tables):

- Aberdeen .... dep
- Stonehaven ....
- Laurencekirk ....
- Bridge of Dun ....
- Forfar ....
- Alyth Junction ....
- Coupar Angus ....
- 35 Inverness ....
- Dundee (Tay B'dge) dep
- Dundee (West) ....
- Invergowrie ....
- Errol ....
- Perth (Princes St.) .. arr
- Perth .... arr
- Perth .... dep
- Comrie ....
- Crieff ....
- Pittenzie Halt. ....
- Highlandman ....
- Strageath Halt. ....
- Muthill ....
- Tullibardine ....
- Gleneagles ....
- Dunblane ....
- Bridge of Allan ....
- Stirling .... arr
- Larbert. ....
- 20 Falkirk (Grahamston) arr
- 20 Edinburgh (Prin. St.)..
- Greenhill ....
- Cumbernauld ....
- Coatbridge (Cen.) .. dep
- Glasgow (Buch. St.).. arr

Named trains referenced: THE GRAMPIAN, THE GRANITE CITY, THE SAINT MUNGO.

Notes and connections referenced include:
- TC Alloa dep 5 52 pm (Table 28)
- Runs 29th June to 31st August inclusive
- MB Dundee to Glasgow
- Dep Arbroath 2 50, Carnoustie 3 3, Monifieth 3 14, Broughty Ferry 3 21 pm (Table 27)
- Runs 29th June to 24th August incl. TC Arbroath to Glasgow
- TC Grangemouth dep 5 1 pm (Table 19)
- MB Aberdeen to Glasgow
- RC and TC Aberdeen to Edinburgh (Waverley)
- TC Arbroath dep 2 29 pm (Table 27)
- TC Aberdeen to Edinburgh (Waverley)
- TC from Callander dep 4 0 pm
- TC Oban dep 12 40 pm to Edinburgh (Table 33)
- Commences 13th July
- RC Inverness to Perth
- TC Inverness to Glasgow

- TC Aberdeen to Edinburgh (Waverley)
- MB Observation Car Oban dep 5 30 pm to Glasgow and Edinburgh
- TC Oban dep 5 30 pm to Glasgow
- TC Inverness to Glasgow
- RB Inverness Saturdays only, Aviemore to Glasgow, Aviemore to Glasgow Saturdays except
- TC Inverness to Glasgow, RB Aviemore to Glasgow
- Runs 29th June to 31st August inclusive
- THE GRANITE CITY RC Aberdeen to Glasgow
- RB Aberdeen to Glasgow on 22nd June and 7th September
- RB Dundee to Glasgow on 22nd June and 7th September
- TC Callander dep 6 20 pm to Edinburgh (Table 33)
- RC and TC Aberdeen to Edinburgh (Waverley)
- TC Perth to Edinburgh
- Limited accommodation from Aberdeen to Perth
- Limited accommodation from Aberdeen to Perth for bicycles, heavy luggage or bicycles

---

Table 32—continued

ABERDEEN, DUNDEE, PERTH, STIRLING, EDINBURGH (Princes Street), and GLASGOW (Buchanan Street)

Week Days—continued

Named trains referenced: THE SAINT MUNGO, THE SAINT MUNGO.

Notes and connections referenced include:
- TC Grangemouth dep 12 4 pm (Table 19)
- TC Arbroath dep 10 12 am (Table 27)
- RC Aberdeen to Glasgow
- TC Oban dep 9 30 am to Glasgow (Table 33)
- TC Aberdeen to Edinburgh (Waverley)
- RC, MB and TC Perth to London (Euston)
- TC Aberdeen to London (Euston) arr 9 57 pm except Saturdays
- RB Dundee to Glasgow on Saturdays from 29th June to 31st August incl.
- TC Dundee to Edinburgh

- TC Arbroath dep 11 45 am (Table 27)
- TC Arbroath dep 11 48 am (Table 27)
- TC Callander dep 1 28 pm to Glasgow (Table 33)
- RC and TC Oban dep 11 45 am to Glasgow (Table 33)
- TC Oban dep 11 45 am to Glasgow (Table 33)
- RC and TC Oban dep 11 45 am to Glasgow
- TC Aberdeen to Edinburgh (Waverley)
- MB Dundee to Glasgow
- RC Oban to Glasgow except Saturdays
- TC Oban to Edinburgh except on Saturdays commencing 13th July
- TC Oban dep 12 5 pm to Glasgow (Table 33)
- TC Inverness to Glasgow
- Commences 29th June

Table 32—continued

ABERDEEN, DUNDEE, PERTH, STIRLING, EDINBURGH (Princes Street) and GLASGOW (Buchanan Street)

Sundays—continued

Stations (reading down):

Aberdeen ... dep
Stonehaven
Laurencekirk
Bridge of Dun
Forfar
Alyth Junction
Coupar Angus
35 Inverness
Dundee (Tay B'dge) dep
Dundee (West) ... dep
Invergowrie
Errol
Perth (Princes St.) ... arr
Perth ... dep
Comrie
Crieff
Pittenzie Halt
Highlandman
Strageath Halt
Muthill
Tullibardine
Gleneagles
Dunblane
Bridge of Allan
Stirling ... arr
Larbert
20 Falkirk (Grahamston) arr
20 Edinburgh (Prin. St.)
Greenhill
Cumbernauld
Coatbridge (Cen.) ... dep
Glasgow (Buch. St.) ... arr

NOTES

A Except Mondays
am Stops on notice only to take up
B Arr 8 0 am Saturday mornings
8 5 am Sunday mornings
C Diesel service except on Saturdays
D Diesel Service
E or E Except Saturdays
F Fridays only
g Calls Carnoustie on 23rd June
only
On Saturdays from 13th July arr
4 23 pm
H Saturdays only and commences 13th
July
J Arr 7 16 pm on Fridays and Saturdays
Except Saturday and Sunday nights
K Conveys passengers beyond Edinburgh
only

MB Miniature Buffet Car
n noon
p pm
Q Arr Glasgow (Queen Street)
RB Buffet Car
RC Restaurant Car
S or S Saturdays only
SC Sleeping Car
T Stops if required to set down on
notice to the guard and to take up
when there are passengers on the
platform

TC Through Carriages
U Does not convey Aberdeen to
Stonehaven passengers. On Fridays
28th June to 30th August conveys
seating passengers for South of York
only and Carlisle and beyond, also
passengers to Leuchars Jn. Cupar
and Inverkeithing
v Calls to set down only
W Dep Falkirk (Grahamston)
Waverley Station
x am. Central Station
y Arr Waverley Station. Change at
Polmont
Z Second class only

For LOCAL TRAINS and intermediate stations between Aberdeen and Edinburgh, (Wav.) see Table 2)

For OTHER TRAINS between Aberdeen and Edinburgh, see Table 27—Perth and Edinburgh, Table 27—Stirling
and Edinburgh, Table 27—Aberdeen and Glasgow, Table 27

Table 32—continued

ABERDEEN, DUNDEE, PERTH, STIRLING, EDINBURGH (Princes Street) and GLASGOW (Buchanan Street)

Week Days—continued

Stations (reading down):

Aberdeen ... dep
Stonehaven
Laurencekirk
Bridge of Dun
Forfar
Alyth Junction
Coupar Angus
35 Inverness
Dundee (Tay B'dge) dep
Dundee (West) ... dep
Invergowrie
Errol
Perth (Princes St.) ... arr
Perth ... dep
Comrie
Crieff
Pittenzie Halt
Highlandman
Strageath Halt
Muthill
Tullibardine
Gleneagles
Dunblane
Bridge of Allan
Stirling ... arr
Larbert
20 Falkirk (Grahamston) arr
20 Edinburgh (Prin. St.)
Greenhill
Cumbernauld
Coatbridge (Cen.) ... dep
Glasgow (Buch. St.) ... arr

Sundays

Aberdeen ... dep
Stonehaven
Laurencekirk
Bridge of Dun
Forfar
Alyth Junction
Coupar Angus
35 Inverness
Dundee (Tay B'dge) dep
Dundee (West) ... dep
Invergowrie
Errol
Perth (Princes St.) ... arr
Perth ... dep
Comrie
Crieff
Pittenzie Halt
Highlandman
Strageath Halt
Muthill
Tullibardine
Gleneagles
Dunblane
Bridge of Allan
Stirling ... arr
Larbert
20 Falkirk (Grahamston) arr
20 Edinburgh (Prin. St.)
Greenhill
Cumbernauld
Coatbridge (Cen.) ... dep
Glasgow (Buch. St.) ... arr

For Notes, see page 337

1 Farewells are said at Buchanan Street o
31st August 1965 as the hands of the cloc
approach departure time and Class A
Pacific No. 60026, *Miles Beevor,* is read
to leave at the head of 'The Saint Mungo
the 5.30pm express to Aberdeen. On th
left, one of the named Class B1 4-6-0s No
61244, *Strang Steel,* waits to follow wit
the 5.35pm to Dunblane. An interestin
feature in this picture is the woode
walkway between the tracks, provided fo
the convenience of operating staff. *Mile
Beevor* was built in 1937, and original
named *Kestrel:* it was renamed i
November 1947. During its career it wa
based at no fewer than eight differen
sheds, but spent most of its time in BR day
at Kings Cross. In April 1964 it wa
transferred to Aberdeen Ferryhill depot, an
was withdrawn at Perth in December of th
following year. Components from No
60026 were later used by Crewe Work
during the restoration of No. 60007 as No
4498, *Sir Nigel Gresley.* *W. A. C. Smit*

Glasgow Buchanan Street

The journey begins at Glasgow's dingy Buchanan Street station, the least impressive of the city's main termini. It was opene
by the Caledonian Railway (CR) on 1st November 1849, replacing the original terminus at Glebe Street, St. Rollox, inherite
from the Glasgow, Garnkirk and Coatbridge Railway which the Caledonian had absorbed in 1846. Glebe Street statio
opened on 27th September 1831, was the first in the city, but its isolated location well away from the city centre led to it
early demise. Access to Buchanan Street station involved constructing a new line from Milton Junction, more than two mile
away, which dropped down through St. Rollox and underneath the Forth and Clyde canal. This involved some considerabl
gradients for trains leaving Glasgow, with an initial climb, partially in a tunnel, as steep as 1 in 79, although gradients wer
moderated to 1 in 125 after two and a half miles at Milton Junction. For the first thirty years of its existence Buchana
Street station was used by the CR's Anglo-Scottish services until Central Station was brought into use on 1st August 1879.

In 1932 the station was rebuilt by the LMSR. The main buildings were constructed of timber on a steel frame. Th
station frontage was horizontally boarded with classical wooden pilasters, and a new glass roofed concourse was provided
The platforms had to make do with secondhand awnings removed from the then recently closed station of Ardrossan North
In more recent years trains to and from the south sometimes again used Buchanan Street as a result of engineering works, bu
its main purpose was as the Glasgow terminus of services to Aberdeen, Oban, and Inverness. The station closed on 7t
November 1966 when its remaining services were diverted to Queen Street. Since that time the site, which included a good
depot reputed to be the largest in Scotland, has been partially redeveloped and it is difficult to believe a sizeable railwa
establishment once existed there. A link with the past is, however, maintained as ScotRail House (originally Buchanan Hous
stands on part of the former station site.

2 Smoke and steam blow around in the
wind obscuring the background as No.
60026, *Miles Beevor,* pulls out from
Buchanan Street with the 5.30pm
express to Aberdeen. This photograph
was taken on 25th April 1964, less
than a fortnight after the locomotive's
transfer to Aberdeen. On the left BR
Standard Class 5 No. 73152 stands at
the head of the 5.35 pm to Dunblane.
W. A. C. Smith

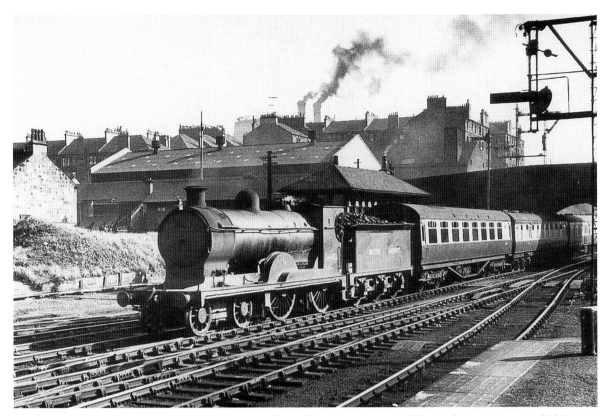

3 A former CR 4-4-0, No. 54483, brings the 8.55am from Stepps into Buchanan Street station on 3rd August 1953. The rake of coaches includes an LNER vehicle behind the engine, a twelve-wheeled LMSR restaurant car and BR Standard brake coach. Note the precariously-perched lampman who is attending to a signal behind the bridge.
P. Hay

Watched by a large contingent of enthusiasts, No. 60031, *Golden Plover,* makes a dramatic exit from Buchanan Street station with the 6.15pm to Dundee on 19th April 1965. Though the A4s certainly attracted large numbers of enthusiasts, the number present on this occasion was probably swollen by many who had just alighted from a railtour at an adjacent platform. The vigorous start being made by the Pacific's driver cannot be dismissed as simply 'playing to the gallery'. The lengthy 3¼ miles climb out of Glasgow, some of it in tunnel, necessitated a brisk getaway.
J. J. Smith

5 On the beautifully clear morning of 20th July 1966 Class A4 No. 60034, *Lord Faringdon,* leaves Buchanan Street station at th commencement of its three-hour run to the Granite City in charge of the 8.25am departure, 'The Grampian'. The dilapidated condition the station's platform awnings and surrounding area will be noted. It is likely that No. 60034 was the only member of its class active at th time, as sister locomotives Nos. 60019/24 spent most of that month out of action, much to the disappointment of many enthusiasts wh made the pilgrimage to Scotland to see the A4s. Some compensation was, however, provided by Class A2 Pacific No. 60532, *Blue Pete* which regularly headed the 1.30pm Aberdeen-Glasgow and 11.2pm return. *D. Hum*

6 Class A2 Pacific No. 6053 *Blue Peter,* gets to grips with th rising gradient away fro Buchanan Street as it depart with the 8.25am to Aberdeen o 4th July 1966.

D. Hum

No. 60034, *Lord Faringdon,* leaving the 8.25am to Aberdeen completes [thi]s panoramic view of the approaches to [th]e terminus. The new building under [co]nstruction in the background is [Bu]chanan House, later ScotRail House, [an]d following the demolition of the [sta]tion in 1967 other buildings were built [on] the site. The area in the foreground [re]mains derelict however, the retaining [wa]ll plus the tunnel entrance still being [ex]tant in early 1992, twenty-five years [aft]er closure! The ground behind the rear [of] the train is the site of the former [Bu]chanan Street engine shed which is [bel]ieved to have been demolished in the [19]40s. *D. Hume*

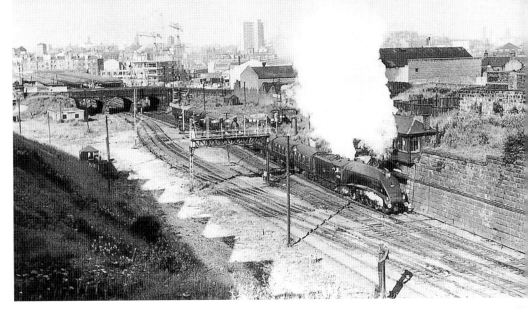

Class V2 2-6-2 No. 60816 approaches the site of St. Rollox station on 17th May 1964 in charge of the 7.15pm Glasgow to Dundee [tr]ain. This location is about one mile from Buchanan Street and the line is still climbing at a gradient of 1 in 79. There was formerly a [ch]emical works on a nearby site and its effluent appears to have created a man-made wasteland, known locally as the 'soda wastes'. [O]blivious to the dangers, a number of children are just discernible using the area as a playground. The bridge in the background carried the [Po]rt Dundas goods line. *D. Hume*

9 St. Rollox works (on the right) is well known as the CR's locomotive shops, but perhaps less widely known is the fact that there was an adjacent station, also named St. Rollox. On 4th July 1962 Class 5 No. 45084 is seen pausing at the head of the 5.1pm Grangemouth - Glasgow train. Sighthill freight depot is just in view on the left. Nowadays part of the former works is famous as the headquarters of MC Metal Processing Ltd., a firm of scrap merchants who break up large quantities of redundant locomotives and coaches. St. Rollox station closed on 5th November 1962. *D. Hume*

10 A very grimy Class 5, No. 44704, passes the lofty signal box at Germiston Junction on 12th July 1966 with the 5.50pm Buchanan Street to Stirling train. The tracks going off to the right led to Balornock Junction and Rutherglen. Note the quite complicated track layout, a legacy of the days before standardisation of permanent way components. *D. Hume*

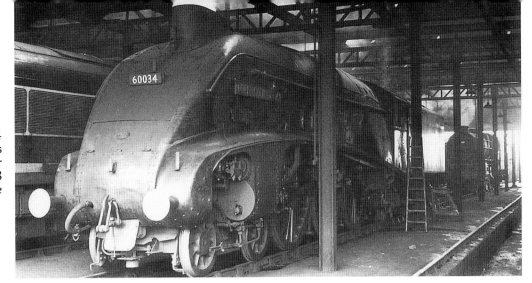

On 24th April 1966, Class A4 No. 60034, *Lord Faringdon,* was photographed in the gloomy interior of St. Rollox shed. Class 5 No. 44998 stands on the same road.   *D. Hume*

St. Rollox Shed

St. Rollox shed was opened in November 1916 and replaced two much earlier CR establishments at Buchanan Street and at St. Rollox works which dated from 1851 and 1856 respectively. Compared to the notoriously cramped and primitive sheds it replaced St. Rollox (which was generally known as Balornock prior to nationalisation) was spacious and well laid out. The depot was located in the Provanmill district and situated on a large site adjacent to the main line serving Buchanan Street station. It was surrounded by either railway lines or, on one side, Broomfield Road, but these did not restrict operations. The twelve road brick-built building also had two repair bays. A wooden coaling stage, the coaling road of which adjoined the main line tracks, was also provided. The depot was well equipped with repair facilities, although these fell short of the equipment available at Polmadie, across the river. A seventy feet-long Ransomes and Rapier turntable was ordered at a cost of £685, and this piece of machinery lasted through to closure. Naturally, being a CR shed, St. Rollox was largely inhabited for the first twenty or so years of its existence by CR locomotive types, and indeed for a time during the mid-1930s it boasted a total of eighteen CR 4-6-0s of six different classes! Towards the end of the 1930s this dominance by CR types began to wane as more and more Stanier Class 5s became available, so that by the time of nationalisation all the pre-grouping 4-6-0s had disappeared and the shed had twenty-eight Class 5s on its books. In the 1950s St. Rollox was the home of all four of the named Class 5s for a time until two were transferred south of the border in March 1957. Another development during that year was the allocation of ten Caprotti-fitted BR Standard Class 5s. In 1962 a pair of *ex*-LNER A4 4-6-2s – Nos. 60027, *Merlin,* and 60031, *Golden Plover* – were allocated to St. Rollox as a result of a decision to speed up the Glasgow – Aberdeen services. At that time the Scottish Region was experiencing considerable teething troubles with its temperamental diesel fleet and these machines were simply not deemed reliable enough to be entrusted with the new services, so displaced Pacifics were drafted in. The fact that *ex*-LNER locomotives were moved to a shed with a long tradition of LMSR practice was quite remarkable. Later, more former LNER locomotive types, principally A3, V2 and B1 classes, became regular visitors to the depot and in many ways the final few years of St. Rollox shed's existence were the most interesting from the enthusiast's point of view. After a career lasting almost exactly fifty years the depot closed on 7th November 1966. During this time the shed remained almost completely unchanged, even the wooden coal stage surviving intact. The site of the shed remained unoccupied following demolition of the buildings, but the whole area has recently been subjected to considerable upheaval due to construction of a vast road scheme. Happily, at least the Glasgow Queen Street to Cumbernauld trains survive!

A sad moment at St. Rollox as No. 60019, *Bittern,* tops up its tender before moving off shed to Buchanan Street to work the Scottish Region's commemorative last A4 run to Aberdeen on 3rd September 1966. Note the white buffers!   *M. S. Burns*

13 During 1959 Glasgow Central was in the throes of resignalling and on Sundays Anglo-Scottish main-line services were diverted to Buchanan Street. Here 'Princess Royal' Pacific No. 46201, *Princess Elizabeth,* is seen passing St. Rollox depot with the empty coaches to form a Glasgow to Birmingham train on 12th April. The line-up on the 'coaling-up' road includes visiting celebrities in the form of a BR Standard 'Clan' 4-6-2 and 'Princess Coronation' Pacific No. 46228, *Duchess of Rutland.* A new road has recently been constructed in this area, involving massive earthworks which have altered the topography beyond recognition. *G. W. Morrison*

14 Class 5 No. 45473 and Class A4 No. 60007, *Sir Nigel Gresley,* await their next turns of duty at St. Rollox shed in August 1964. No. 60007, one of the most famous A4s of all, was built at Doncaster in 1937. For most of its career it was shedded at London, Kings Cross, and when that depot closed in June 1963 No. 60007 was transferred briefly to New England, Peterborough shed. In October 1963 No. 60007 moved to Scotland and was officially allocated to St. Margarets shed, Edinburgh. In reality it was put into store across the city at Dalry Road shed before being put back into traffic at Aberdeen on 20th July 1964. It worked on the Glasgow three-hour services until withdrawn in February 1966 for preservation, and is now a regular sight on railtours. *I. S. Krause*

BR Standard Class 5 No. 73146 passes its home shed hauling a lengthy Buchanan Street to Aberdeen express on 20th February 1965.

J. L. Stevenson

On 10th May 1966 Caprotti-fitted Standard Class 5 No. 73150 passes Robroyston West, on the outskirts of Glasgow, with the 5.35pm Buchanan Street to Dunblane train.

D. Hume

17 Class 5 No. 45084 enters Cumbernauld station with a Glasgow-bound train on 10th August 1965. Judging by the appearance passengers waiting on the platform it would appear to be a morning commuter service. The station here has since been rebuilt in a rath soulless modern style.

John Go.

Cumbernauld

The section of route from Gartsherrie to Greenhill, which passes through Cumbernauld, was opened for traffic on 7th Augu 1848 and was the final link in the 500 mile main line between London Euston and Dubton Junction, near Montrose, via t West Coast route. The final section of track from Dubton to Aberdeen was opened for traffic two years later. Until t closure of Glasgow Buchanan Street station in November 1966, Cumbernauld was mainly served by services to and fro Stirling and north thereof, but when these were rerouted into Queen Street station only a suburban service connecting t town with Glasgow remained. The town's passenger service to the north was withdrawn, but London-Perth express continued to pass through without stopping; thus Cumbernauld found itself in the strange position of possessing a throug station offering a passenger service only in one direction. In more recent years InterCity trains have been rerouted to run v Edinburgh but the line north of Cumbernauld remains open for freight.

18 The 3.30pm Aberdeen-Glasgo train passes Cumbernauld signal b with Class 5 No. 44797 in charge 28th July 1966. The box is still in use the time of writing, while the siding the left is used as a shunting neck f terminating trains from Glasgow.

D. Hun

Just north of Cumbernauld the route passes through the thickly-wooded Cumbernauld Glen – a most attractive stretch of line. Here BR Standard 'Clan' Pacific No. 72007, *Clan Mackintosh,* threads past the tree-lined slopes with a northbound passenger train on 31st July 1964. The photographer recorded the precise time at which his picture was taken, 4.5pm, so it is reasonable to assume that the train is the 25am Crewe to Aberdeen which was due to leave Coatbridge Central at 3.41pm. No. 72007 had a short career: it was built at Crewe in bruary 1952 and lasted only fourteen years in service until it was condemned in December 1965. The two coaches visible are passenger brake vans (BGs) the first being of LMSR design, while the following vehicle is a BR Standard type. *P. S. Leavens*

Cumbernauld Glen

20 A grimy Class WD 2-8-0 No. 90489 heads north through Cumbernauld Glen with a freight train on 20th April 1965. *D. E. Gouldthorp*

21 On the bright spring morning of 20th April 1965 No. 60019, *Bittern,* climbs through Cumbernauld Glen in charge of the 7.10a from Aberdeen. No. 60019 entered traffic in December 1937 and was allocated to Heaton, Newcastle, shed. It was transferred Gateshead in March 1943: *Bittern* spent twenty years there before being moved to Edinburgh St. Margarets shed in October 1963. month later it was on the move again, this time to Ferryhill where it remained for the rest of its working life. No. 60019 was fortunate receive a heavy intermediate overhaul at Darlington in March 1965, shortly before this picture was taken, which doubtless accounted for survival right to the end of A4 operation. *Bittern* was one of the best, and therefore most popular, performers of Ferryhill's A4 stud ar subsequently survived into preservation, though it is not in working order at the time of writing. *D. E. Gouldthor*

2 Class A2 Pacific No. 60532, *Blue Peter,* makes a fine sight as it heads for Glasgow on the last stage of its journey from Aberdeen ~~d~~ring July 1966. Though not apparent from the seemingly effortless progress being made by No. 60532, the line is actually climbing ~~to~~wards Glasgow on a 1 in 128 gradient which continues until the summit is reached at Cumbernauld station, from where the line generally ~~de~~scends towards Glasgow.

M. S. Burns

3 Class 2MT 2-6-0 No. 46460, of ~~G~~rangemouth shed, rattles past Larbert ~~Ju~~nction with a short local freight working on ~~18t~~h August 1964. The line from Edinburgh, via ~~F~~alkirk Grahamston, joins the main Glasgow to ~~A~~berdeen route at this point.   *W. S. Sellar*

24 This view of Larbert stati with a Glasgow-bound expr running in, was taken on 8th J 1965. Motive power is provi by Caprotti-fitted Standard Clas No. 73148, which was one c batch of ten of these machi sent to St. Rollox shed when n in 1957. They remained there their working lives and prov excellent performers on t Aberdeen road, although rat overshadowed by the other, m illustrious, locomotive clas employed on the route. Larb station has since been rebuilt modern 'steel and glass' style.
Martin S. We

Larbert

The main line through Larbert was opened by the Scottish Central Railway (SCR) on 3rd March 1848, with a service Stirling. Soon afterwards, by 23rd May, the line was opened throughout to Perth. Initially the railway company was ridicul because the southern end of its line terminated in an empty field at Greenhill. The CR was busy building its northe extension, however, and in August 1848 the two lines were joined end to end, thus giving access to the Glasgow area, t industrial county of Lanarkshire, and the south. Immediately south of Larbert two triangular junctions were constructed. T line which runs off in an easterly direction was built by the Stirlingshire Midland Junction Company which was authorised July 1846 to construct a line from Polmont, on the Edinburgh and Glasgow Railway, to a junction with the SCR just outsi Larbert. This gave Edinburgh a direct link to Stirling and Perth. The other, westerly, route was a minor branch to Denr opened in 1858, which later connected with the Kelvin Valley Railway, and was amalgamated with the North British Railw (NBR). To the north of Larbert a line to Alloa was opened in July 1852. A secondary line from Alloa to Kinross was a use diversionary route for Glasgow – Perth trains as it gave direct access to Perth via Glenfarg. This scenic line, which was at o time used by the NBR's trains from Glasgow to Perth, was closed totally in June 1964. The main line north of Larbe involves a 1 in 126 climb for two miles up to a minor summit at Plean, after which it drops down on a similar gradie towards Stirling.

25 This scene at the north end of Larb station on 11th June 1966 depicts commendably clean Class 5, No. 44703, Ferryhill shed, entering the up platfo hauling the 1.30pm *ex*-Aberdeen. T centre roads have since disappeared, but t station remains semaphore signalled, wi Larbert North signal box (behind the seco coach of the train) still very much in use. fact this area is a happy hunting ground f signalling aficionados, because the triangul junction with the Falkirk line at Carmuirs, little over a mile south of here, is among t last of its type in Great Britain to b mechanically signalled, with boxes at each the three junctions.
J. L. Stevenso

26 The wide variety of scenery through which the Glasgow-Aberdeen route passes is well known, but here, just south of Stirling, at Bannockburn, a colliery waste tip is the most prominent feature, apart from the distant hills. These blots on the countryside, once so common throughout the mining areas of Great Britain, are a rapidly disappearing feature, so perhaps one should be saved for posterity! For the record, the train in view is a southbound express, with Class 5 No. 44797 in charge, and the picture was taken on 31st May 1966.

Martin S. Welch

27 The low winter sunshine provides beautiful lighting for this picture of Class A4 Pacific No. 60034, *Lord Faringdon,* as it climbs away from Stirling, near St. Ninian's crossing. The train is the 1.30pm from Aberdeen to Glasgow and the date is 12th March 1966.

D. Hume

Stirling Shed

Stirling shed, designed for the Scottish Central Railway in 1850, was a substantial stone building of massive proportions.
replaced a wooden-built structure which is purported to have stood at the southern end of the station. The site, south of tl
station on the east side of the line, was rather cramped and various alternative plans were drawn up. The depot was origina
single-ended, but in 1896 it became possible to extend the restricted site southwards, so the opportunity was taken to conve
it into a through shed, a process made easier by the fact that the 'terminal' end had been built with archways from the outse
At the same time various buildings, housing mess rooms and stores offices, were relocated and the shed's 50ft turntab
moved to its southernmost extremity. Between 1947 and 1953 the original arches, which had been such a distinctive ar
decorative feature of the building, were removed when repairs were needed on the southern end of the shed. During LMS
days very little was done to modernise the depot's facilities, but early in the BR administration an adjoining site becam
available for development, and a plan of expansion for the shed was put into effect. A new roundhouse was proposed, serve
by a seventy-feet diameter turntable removed from Polmadie shed. The turntable was installed, served by two access road
and an office block and machine shop were built, but they were the only parts of the plan implemented. Throughout i
existence Stirling shed kept a distinctly 'Caledonian' atmosphere, and even as late as the mid-1950s more than half i
allocation was made up of *ex*-CR locomotives, mostly shunting types. At that time there were no fewer than twelve CR 0-6-0
on its books. Towards the end, diesel shunters ousted many of their steam counterparts, and various types of main-lir
diesels stabled at the depot; indeed by 1965 its allocation of a mere ten locomotives consisted of six steam, and four diese
Closure to steam traction came on 13th June 1966. The site of Stirling shed is still visible today, but the noise and bustle
this once busy depot have gone for ever.

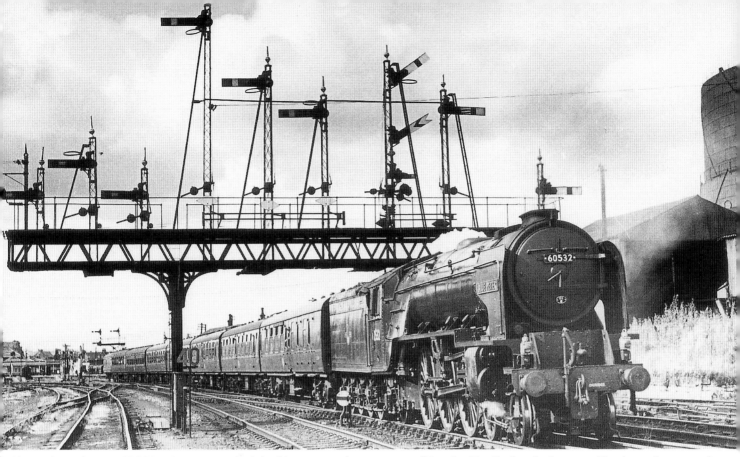

Class A2 Pacific No. 60532, *Blue Peter,* which had been a regular occupant of Dundee Tay Bridge shed on stand-by duties for most of the year, suddenly came into its own in the summer of 1966 when it was transferred to Aberdeen Ferryhill. Previously its workings had been predictable, but Ferryhill, by this time very short of motive power for their steam turns, gave No. 60532 a regular diagram on the 30pm to Glasgow and 11.2pm return. During its very brief spell there it quickly earned an excellent reputation as a powerful and very free-running machine. Note the engine is displaying a '61B' shed allocation plate, but the buffer-beam still shows its previous home shed, undee'. Fortunately *Blue Peter* was preserved and is currently in regular use on railtours, but sadly the magnificent signal gantry is no more. It was taken out of use in February, 1985.   *M. S. Burns*

Southbound from Stirling

31 The vigilant driver of No. 60009, *Union of South Africa,* appears to be checking that the road ahead is clear of permanent-way staff who are just visible in the distance. The train is 'The Bon Accord' (7.10am *ex*-Aberdeen) and this photograph was taken on 22nd April 1965.   *J. S. Whiteley*

32 BR Standard 'Britannia' Pacifics had a number of turns between Carlisle and Perth, and on occasions it was not unknown for them to work through to Aberdeen. In this view No. 70003, *John Bunyan,* is seen pulling out of Stirling at the head of the 2.45pm Perth to Carstairs parcels train on 5th May 1965. Stirling station can be glimpsed in the background, while the tracks leading to the locomotive shed are on the right. The locomotive began its life on the former Great Eastern main line working expresses from Liverpool Street to Norwich, during which time it was doubtless maintained in exemplary condition, in sad contrast to its appalling exterior state in this picture. In addition, like nearly all the 'Britannias' by this time, it is running without nameplates.
W. S. Sellar

33 Class A2 No. 60527, *Sun Chariot,* makes a spirited departure from Stirling in charge of the 1.30pm Aberdeen to Glasgow train on 8th June 1963. Stirling Middle signal box is still in use at the time of writing and must now rank as one of the largest mechanical boxes remaining in Great Britain.
W. A. C. Smith

34 *Opposite:* Snow has alrea partially covered the point roddi and it looks as though Stirli station is about to be engulfed Class 5 No. 45084 pulls out with Glasgow-bound train during blizzard in February 1966. N 45084 was one of a batch of fi engines of this class built in 19: by Vulcan Foundry, and w withdrawn in November 1966.
C. E. West

35 On 8th June 1965 Class 5 No. 45423, of Stirling shed, prepares to depart with a southbound unidentified local train. Th train is standing at one of the platforms on the eastern side of the station which, at least in the author's experience, were rare used. Certainly they offer very little protection from the weather, unlike the platforms in the 'main' part of the station, both which have canopies. No. 45423 was built by Armstrong Whitworth in 1937, and lasted until May 1967. *Martin S. Wel*

Stirling

For a few months in the spring of 1848 Stirling was the northern terminus of the SCR's line. This situation did n last long, however, as connection was soon made with Perth, followed two months later by the opening of the la section of the route from London. Stirling station is possibly the most attractive on the Glasgow – Aberdeen rout and arguably in the whole of Scotland. The present structures and layout date from 1915 when they replaced th previous facilities which had become seriously inadequate. The main building, located on the down side, was bui with a grey stone castellated frontage leading to a particularly fine semi-circular shaped circulating area of which th inner arc was filled by the booking office. Other station offices lead off from the other curve of the circulating are which is protected by a fully glazed roof supported by artistic ironwork and stanchions.

Operationally, the station was divided in two before nationalisation with the LMSR owning and staffing the statio and providing the vast majority of trains which used the principal platforms. Generally LNER trains from Edinburg via the Forth Bridge, and Fife, used the easternmost platforms which were reached independently of the LMSR line the LNER even had a separate bridge across the River Forth. These services used the route originally constructed b the Stirling and Dunfermline Railway which opened in July 1852. There was also a route west from Stirling, th former Forth and Clyde Railway, which extended over thirty miles to Balloch on the shores of Loch Lomond. Th line was remote from any centres of population and was largely closed in 1934, although a section did linger on unt 1951. At one time through coaches were operated by the LNER from Edinburgh to Balloch and Aberfoyle vi Stirling as part of their 'Trossach Tours'.

36 Class A4 No. 60019, *Bittern*, leave Stirling with the 8.25am Buchanan Stree Aberdeen on 2nd June 1966. This train, an the 5.15pm *ex*-Aberdeen return working, ha been diesel-worked for some time, and the reversion to steam operation from 18th Apr 1966 was a welcome, if unexpectec development. *Bittern* had the virtu: monopoly of this diagram for many weeks u to the end of June but, like the other tw remaining Class A4s, Nos. 60024/34, spent much of July out of action. No. 6001 was under repair at Ferryhill shed, its retur to service apparently being delayed by th annual holiday at Inverurie works which wa expected to provide some material. The top floor bedrooms at the Station Hotel (on th extreme right) appear to offer an exceller vantage point from where to observe A activity. *Martin S. Welch*

37 Class A4 No. 60019, *Bittern,* lays a massive smoke screen as it leaves Stirling with 'The Saint Mungo', the 5.30pm from Glasgow, on 16th July 1965. *S. C. Nash*

38 Class A2 Pacific No. 60530, *Sayajirao,* gets away briskly from Stirling with the 6.15pm Glasgow-Dundee train on 31st August 1965. This locomotive was turned out specially to work a trip to and from Glasgow on this day. The weather appears perfect for photography, the locomotive making a splendid sight in the evening sunshine. On the left, part of the former NBR Shore Road locomotive shed is visible. *W. A. C. Smith*

39 Situated just under three miles north of Stirling is Bridge of Allan station, from where Stanier Class 5 No. 45389 is seen setting off with the 11.10am Stirling to Callander local train on 15th January 1963. This train will travel on the Glasgow-Aberdeen route for exactly five miles, before branching off at Dunblane. Bridge of Allan lost its passenger facilities from 1st November 1965, and the goods yard, part of which is visible on the left, has been developed for commercial use. The old station house remains in use as a private dwelling. A new station was constructed some years ago a few yards to the south of the old station site and enjoys a frequent service to both Edinburgh and Glasgow. *W. S. Sellar*

Despite its modest length of forty-four miles the SCR was not an easy route to construct. North of Stirling, from Bridge of Allan to Kinbuck, there is a continuous climb mostly at 1 in 88, which was needed to avoid very heavy civil engineering work further along the line. The section immediately beyond Stirling follows the course of the meandering Allan Water, but sharp curves were not permitted so contractors Thomas Brassey and James Falshaw (who were later responsible for construction of the Aberdeen to Inverness line) were forced to build numerous lofty embankments and deep cuttings. The Bridge of Allan to Kippenross section involved carving out the steep hillside of the Park of Keir, while parts of the beautiful glen of Kippenross were devastated by heavy forest clearance and diversions of the River Allan. Most of the damage was, however, made good by replanting and the passage of time. In their efforts to build a relatively straight line the surveyors were obliged to cross the Allan Water six times in only five miles! The major engineering work in this area is the 594 yards-long tunnel beneath Kippenross Park, part of which was built by the cut and cover method. Another tunnel was constructed at Ashfield, two miles north of Dunblane, but this 300 yards-long bore was later opened out.

40 The section from just south of Bridge of Allan to just short of Gleneagles is severely graded against northbound trains, and the author well remembers exhilarating runs behind a variety of Class A4s along this stretch of line. The steepest grades occur before Kinbuck and vary in severity from 1 in 78 to a short 1 in 250 section. The worst stretch, just before Dunblane Station, is pictured here with one of St. Rollox shed's fleet of Caprotti-fitted Standard Class 5 forging its way uphill. These machines were exceptionally noisy when working hard, and one can only imagine the deafening blast from the chimney of No. 73145 as it passed the photographer. The train is the 1.15pm Buchanan Street to Dundee West, and the photograph was taken on 23rd May 1964. *W. S. Sellar*

41 The 4.25pm Glasgow-Inverness train approaches Dunblane behind Class 5 No. 44722 on a wet 4th August 1965. *J. Dagley-Morris*

42 Passengers on the upper deck of a local bus on the adjacent road have a bird's-eye view of No. 60034, *Lord Faringdon,* as it pulls out of Dunblane with the 1.30pm *ex*-Aberdeen on 31st May 1966. This attractive town is now the terminating point for 'local' trains from both Edinburgh and Glasgow and enjoys a frequent service to both centres. *Martin S. Welch*

43 Dunblane station provides an appealing setting for this picture of Class 5 No. 45084. The identity of the train is not known, but it is probably the evening rush-hour working from Glasgow which terminated there. The photograph was taken in the mid-1960s.   *M. S. Burns*

Dunblane

44 A young man on the southbound platform waves to the crew of Class 5 No. 45136 as it storms through Dunblane in charge of th 12.15pm Buchanan Street to Aberdeen train on the dull winter's afternoon of 15th February 1964. Passengers on the same platform wa under the canopy for a train to the south which is already signalled. At this time Dunblane was still the junction for the former CR route Oban, but in September 1965 the route was severed by a landslide. Closure between Dunblane and Crianlarich had already been sanctione by the Minister of Transport, so the section north of Callander was abandoned leaving the latter point as the temporary terminus of train from the south until services were withdrawn completely on 1st November 1965, the 'official' closure date. Services from Glasgow to Oba were re-routed to run via Ardlui from that date.   *W. A. C. Smit*

45 Class A4 No. 60034, *Lord Faringdon,* coasts down the hill into Dunblane station with 'The Grampian' (1.30pm from Aberdeen) on 31st May 1966. This train, although named, was not one of the three-hour expresses. It stopped at nearly all the intermediate stations *en route* and took exactly four hours for the journey. No. 60034 was originally constructed as LNER No. 4903, *Peregrine,* at Doncaster Works in July 1938. It was re-named *Lord Faringdon,* after a deputy chairman of the LNER, in March 1948. It spent the greater part of its life at Kings Cross Top shed, but migrated north when steam traction was largely eliminated from the former GNR main line in 1963. It was nominally transferred to St. Margarets shed, Edinburgh, but in reality found itself stored at Bathgate together with another former Kings Cross locomotive, No. 60026, *Miles Beevor.* It was returned to traffic at Aberdeen in May 1964.

Martin S. Welch

46 Between Dunblane and Gleneagles the line makes numerous crossings of the Allan Water, the first of which is pictured here just a few hundred yards north of Dunblane station. The Allan Water is a tributary of the more famous River Forth. The Class 5, No. 44925, is hauling the 10.35am (SO) Blackpool to Aberdeen train on 5th August 1961. Note the composition of the train, those vehicles visible all being of LMSR design, including a superb restaurant car which is the fourth coach behind the locomotive. No. 44925 was in service for twenty years from February 1946 to September 1966.

W. A. C. Smith

47 A beautifully clean locomotive, superb low evening lighting conditions and, of course, a carefully chosen location combine to produce a memorable photograph of No. 60530, *Sayajirao,* as it heads towards its next station stop at Gleneagles with the 6.15pm Glasgow-Dundee on 1st September 1965. The picture was taken north of Dunblane, as the train emerges from a short tunnel which has since been opened out. The Allan Water is in the foreground. *D. E. Gouldthorp*

48 A northbound train makes a fine sight as it heads away from Dunblane in 1966. Motive power is provided by Class 5 No. 44931, which is in very presentable external condition. *M. S. Burns*

9 Maximum effort is exerted by Caprotti Standard Class 5 No. 73151 as it lifts the 5.0pm Glasgow-Dundee up the 1 in 88 gradient ~~towards~~ Kinbuck, at which point a level section is reached. This lasts for two miles before climbing is resumed – albeit on more moderate grades ~~until~~ just short of Gleneagles station. The author will never forget a number of rousing journeys behind these machines, the performance ~~of~~ which was consistently impressive. It is a pity the fine work undertaken by the 'Caprottis' was never given full recognition. This picture ~~was~~ taken on 31st August 1965.

D. E. Gouldthorp

0 The former LMSR 'Princess ~~C~~oronation' class Pacifics continued ~~to~~ work from Carlisle to Perth until ~~th~~e premature withdrawal of the ~~re~~maining members of the class in ~~S~~eptember 1964. Unfortunately, ~~fe~~w photographs of these ~~m~~agnificent machines were ~~su~~bmitted for inclusion in this ~~al~~bum, which the author attributes ~~to~~ their irregular workings, and ~~te~~ndency to work into Perth on ~~ov~~ernight trains from the south, ~~wh~~ich generally arrived before ~~da~~ybreak. In their twilight years it ~~w~~as a melancholy sight to see one ~~of~~ these locomotives reduced to ~~w~~orking a humble van or freight ~~tr~~ain. In this picture, an unkempt ~~No~~. 46226, *Duchess of Norfolk,* ~~sl~~ows for a permanent way slack ~~ju~~st south of Gleneagles station ~~wh~~ilst working a Crewe to Perth ~~pa~~rcels train on 8th June 1963.

J. Dagley-Morris

51 *Bittern* in a blizzard! With snow encrusted on its front end Class A4 No. 60019, *Bittern,* makes a dramatic departure from Gleneagl[es] in a snowstorm on 19th February 1966. The remarkable smoke effect was apparently arranged by the girlfriend of another photograph[er] who was present. She remained at the station and requested the engine crew to 'put on a bit of smoke'. Could she have wished for a mo[re] magnificent response? Gleneagles station is about a mile away from this location. Note the change of gradient; this is the summit of th[e] climb from Stirling and the line now begins its descent towards Perth.

C. E. Westo[n]

52 On 28th August 1964, 'Royal Sc[ot]' 4-6-0 No. 46128, *The Lovat Scou[t],* in disgraceful external condition, leav[es] the long cutting at the south end [of] Gleneagles station with a southbou[nd] fish train in tow.   *P. S. Leave[r]*

53 A Class 5, No. 44795, passes through the deep cutting south of Gleneagles station with a northbound express during the summer of 1964. *R. A. Lissenden*

Gleneagles

54 Gleneagles station is perhaps the most beautifully situated of any on the Glasgow to Aberdeen routes, and in bygone days was known as Crieff Junction. The station was rebuilt in 1919 in what is officially termed 'Edwardian domestic style'. The most interesting features are unusual bow windows on the footbridge towers, and the station's architectural merit has been officially recognised by the granting of listed building status. Most steam enthusiasts would probably regret that a similar accolade was not bestowed upon Class A3 Pacific No. 60042, *Singapore,* which is depicted here leaving with a Glasgow-bound express on 11th May 1963. The loop platform on the left was generally used by Crieff branch trains, and a plume of steam at the far end of the platform indicates that one may be about to depart.

G. W. Morrison

55 Class A4 No. 60024, *Kingfisher,* pulls out of Gleneagles station with 'The Grampian' on 27th May 1966. Note that by this time the Crieff branch, although worked by single diesel railbus vehicles for some time in an effort to economise, had succumbed to closure, and its associated track work had been removed. *J. S. Whiteley*

56 A peep 'behind the scenes' reveals LMSR Ivatt Class 2MT 2-6-0 No. 46403 shunting the goods yard at Gleneagles on 19th October 1963. Class 5 No. 45461 waits to leave the branch platform with the 11.0am to Crieff. Note the dainty shunt signals on the left. *D. Hume*

57 LMSR rebuilt 'Jubilee' 4-6-0 No. 45736, *Phoenix,* waits to leave Gleneagles station in charge of a northbound express on a summer's day in 1964. Note the attractive signals which enhanced this end of the station and also the notice on the left inviting passengers to 'Alight here for Gleneagles Hotel and golf courses'. No. 45736 was one of two 'Jubilees' rebuilt by the LMSR in 1942 with a new 2A type boiler, new exhaust system and other modifications. The 'Royal Scot' class and some 'Patriots' were later fitted with this boiler in preference to further members of the 'Jubilee' class. No. 45736 did not last much longer in traffic, being withdrawn from Carlisle Kingmoor depot in September 1964.

R. A. Lissenden

58 A southbound fish train from Aberdeen approaches Gleneagles station headed by BR Standard 'Britannia' Pacific No. 70011, *Hotspur.* This photograph was taken during the summer of 1964. Regrettably, the 'Britannias' had a very short working life, the example seen here being built at Crewe in May 1951 and lasting in service until the end of 1967.

R. A. Lissenden

60 Auchterarder viaduct is pictured from a different viewpoint in this photograph of 'Royal Scot' Class No. 46128, *The Lovat Scouts*, heading a northbound Anglo-Scottish express, possibly the 9.25am Crewe to Aberdeen train. These locomotives regularly worked through to Perth from Carlisle, but by the summer of 1964, when this photograph was taken, locomotives of this class were rapidly being withdrawn. No. 46128 remained in traffic until May 1965, but by the end of that year this famous class was extinct apart from two preserved examples. *R. A. Lissenden*

59 *Opposite:* In this splendid portrait of No. 60024, *Kingfisher,* the locomotive is seen crossing Auchterarder viaduct with the 1.30pm Aberdeen-Glasgow on 2nd July 1966. The viaduct, which carries the line across a wooded glen, is situated just half a mile south of the former Auchterarder station. *T. Stephens*

Auchterarder

61 Class B1 4-6-0 No. 61180, hauling the 10.0am Aberdeen to Heads of Ayr summer Saturday extra train, passes Auchterarder on 9th July 1966. *C. E. Weston*

63 Taken just a few yards along the line from the previous photograph this view reveals a quite different scene, apart from the brooding hill in the distance. The location is the site of the former Auchterarder station which, in common with many others on the line, lost its passenger service on 11th June 1956. When this portrait was taken, however, almost exactly ten years later on 28th May 1966, much of the former station's infrastructure appears to be remarkably intact. The signal box is still very much in use, and there is at least one wagon in the goods yard, although this may simply have been defective, and detached from a passing freight train rather than present for revenue-earning purposes. The train, hauled by Class 5 No. 44794, is 'The Grampian' from Aberdeen to Glasgow.   *W. A. C. Smith*

62 *Opposite:* Thoughtfully framed by branches of a tree No. 60532, *Blue Peter,* passes Auchterarder powering the 1.30pm Aberdeen to Glasgow train during the summer of 1966. The attractive signal was controlled by the box at the site of the former Auchterarder station which is concealed by drifting smoke from the locomotive. The immediate area of Auchterarder has also been a favourite for photographers due to the close proximity of the Ochil Hills in the background, which otherwise tend to be a rather distant feature along this stretch of line. The peak in view here is the peculiarly named Simpleside Hill which rises to a height of 1,420 feet above sea level. Hills never seen to be very far away on the Aberdeen route, but in the author's opinion this section is the most picturesque on the line.   *M. S. Burns*

64 Just west of Hilton Junction signal box, on 6th June 1963, Class 5 No. 44724 has a good hold of the Glasgow portion of the 3.30pm from Aberdeen, the 'West Coast Postal'. As well as the TPO vans for London, detached at Perth, this train also carried an Edinburgh portion. Usually only three carriages, and at that time running to Princes Street, this portion was detached at Larbert and worked forward from there by a BR Standard 2-6-4T locomotive. On this date, Class A2 Pacific No. 60525, *A. H. Peppercorn,* had worked the four TPO vans away from Perth, but it appears that the crew of No. 44724 were, perhaps optimistically, intent on catching up!
A. G. S. Davies

65 The long journey from Carlisle is almost over for 'Royal Scot' 4-6-0 No. 46128, *The Lovat Scouts,* as it approaches Hilton Junction at the head of the 9.25am *ex*-Crewe on 27th August 1964. Apart from a very short adverse grade at this point, the line descends all the way down from Gleneagles following the valley of the River Earn, which is hidden from view in the middle background. The river flows into the River Tay just a few miles away from this spot. Note the amazing collection of vehicles forming the train, ranging from a couple of BR Standard vans and four-wheeled horsebox at the front, to an LMSR designed full brake van towards the rear. The passenger accommodation is provided by four BR Standard vehicles and a similar number of former LMSR coaches. *P. S. Leavens*

66 A modest load of four TPO vehicles should not over-exert Class A4 No. 60026, *Miles Beevor,* which has just passed Hilton Junction on the long climb to Gleneagles with the up 'West Coast Postal' on 4th June 1965. *J. S. Whiteley*

Approaching Hilton Junction

67 The evening sunshine and wonderful cloud formation, not to mention the elegant lines of No. 60009, *Union of South Africa,* have combined perfectly to produce a gem of a photograph of the 5.30pm Glasgow to Aberdeen approaching Hilton Junction during the summer of 1965. This magnificent sight can still be seen occasionally, when No. 60009 makes one of its forays onto the main line. No. 60009 first saw the light of day as No. 4488, *Osprey,* on 17th April 1937, but its name was changed to *Union of South Africa* before it entered traffic on 29th June. It was allocated to Edinburgh Haymarket shed and remained at that depot for no less than twenty-five years until transferred to Ferryhill to work the Glasgow three-hour trains in May 1962. In 1953 the engine was embellished with a Springbok motif presented by a South African businessman. This is just visible in the photograph half way along the boiler casing. No. 60009 was the last steam locomotive overhauled at Doncaster works, in November 1963, and later achieved another claim to fame when it hauled the last steam-powered train from Kings Cross in October 1964. The locomotive was saved by Mr John Cameron, and occasionally works rail tours over BR tracks, including visits to its former haunt of Aberdeen.

C. E. Weston

68 A fish train, probably the 2.11pm from Aberdeen, sets off for the south past Hilton Junction signal box (the roof of which is just visible) on 27th August 1964. BR Standard 'Britannia' Pacific No. 70003, *John Bunyan,* provides the motive power.

P. S. Leavens

69 Class A2 Pacific No. 60530, *Sayajirao,* emerges from the shadowy cutting at Hilton Junction into bright morning sunlight on 1st September 1965, while hauling the 10.0am from Dundee to Glasgow. The tracks in the foreground at this time connected Perth and Edinburgh by two largely separate routes, one line to Glenfarg and Cowdenbeath and the other line via Ladybank and Thornton Junction. The latter is the only one surviving today, as the heavily-graded Glenfarg line succumbed to closure in early 1970.

D. E. Gouldthorp

70 In this unorthodox view of Hilton Junction, taken near the southern entrance to Moncrieff Tunnel, Class A4 No. 60034, *Lord Faringdon,* is seen approaching with an Aberdeen-bound express in 1965. Hilton Junction signal box is partially visible beyond the junction, where the signal is 'cleared' for the Stirling direction.
J. S. Everitt

71 BR Standard Class 5 No. 73000 leaves Perth hauling an Aberdeen to Glasgow train on 18th September 1965. This locomotive was a rare visitor to Scotland, being based in England at the time. It was presumably 'running-in' after a visit to Cowlairs Works.
D. A. Anderson

72 A local passenger train to Stirling hauled by Class 5 No. 44879 ambles past Perth locomotive depot on 10th May 1958. Built at Crewe Works in May 1945, this engine remained in service until April 1967.   *D. A. Anderson*

Perth Shed

The various railway companies that converged on Perth in the middle of the last century generally built their own premises for the servicing and repair of their locomotive studs. The most important of these engine sheds were the Scottish Midland Junction Railway (SMJR) depot at the north end of Perth station, near the Glasgow Road bridge, and the Scottish Central Railway (SCR) shed which was built where the main line passes under the Edinburgh Road on the south side of the city. A series of mergers took place between some of the railways in the area with the result that, by 1866, the SMJR and SCR had been absorbed into the Caledonian Railway (CR) which inherited the two sheds. The CR lost no time in divesting itself of the former SMJR shed, which was sold to the Highland Railway (HR), and concentrated its activities on the former SCR premises. During the 1850s the SCR had established a major shed and locomotive repair works to the south of Perth station, the former occupying a large area just south of the road bridge on the west side of the line. The generously-proportioned building was built of stone, and was progressively enlarged and improved during later years. The original forty-five feet turntable was replaced by a fifty-feet specimen which itself gave way to a seventy-feet example by 1915. In early LMSR days both the former HR and CR sheds continued to operate independently, but in the 1930s a modernisation scheme was proposed which entailed rebuilding and expanding the former CR premises to enable the old HR depot to be closed. The new shed was constructed of brick, steel and corrugated sheeting, and repair facilities were provided to confirm its status as the principal engine shed for many miles around. A new mechanised coaling plant and turntable built by Cowans Sheldon were also provided, as if to complete the re-equipment, and the 'new' shed opened in May 1938.

The locomotive allocation at Perth shed for many years consisted, as might be expected, of CR locomotives of a variety of designs. The depot allocation of January 1934 confirms this pattern, although a handful of both LMSR 'Compound' 4-4-0s and 'Crab' 2-6-0s were also on the books. In addition the famous CR single No. 123 (then LMSR No. 14010) was also based at Perth and working out its last days prior to withdrawal the following year. It was subsequently preserved and saw considerable use on special trains for a time following restoration to working order in 1957. The introduction of the Stanier Class 5s resulted in the rapid displacement of the CR locomotives from their principal duties, and by the time of nationalisation no fewer than sixty Class 5s were based at Perth, a quite remarkable total. These much-liked and extremely versatile machines even displaced Perth's allocation of Class 8Fs which were sent south to English sheds. During the 1950s an assortment of CR engines continued to find regular employment, the 4-4-0s on local passenger and freight duties along the HR main line, and the 0-4-4Ts on various pilot duties and also the Aberfeldy branch. Towards the end of its career Perth depot, at which many LMSR express locomotive types from south of the border had always been regular visitors, took on an even more cosmopolitan atmosphere following the introduction of Class A4 Pacifics on the Glasgow-Perth-Aberdeen three-hour expresses. Thus, on occasions, it was possible to see 'Princess Coronations' and A4s rubbing buffers on Perth Shed. The depot closed in May 1967 with the elimination of steam traction in Scotland, the final five years of its existence having in many ways proved the most interesting.

3 Perth depot, seen here during the summer of 1965, could easily be mistaken for the former Kings Cross Top Shed such is the glittering line-up of Sir Nigel Gresley's masterpieces. The illusion is slightly spoilt by the presence of at least three Class 5 4-6-0s, but should one complain? In the author's opinion the new lease of life given to so many redundant A4s on the Glasgow to Aberdeen trains was one of the highlights of the final years of British steam traction. The Class A4s pictured here from left to right are Nos. 60009, *Union of South Africa*, 60026, *Miles Beevor*, 60019, *Bittern* and 60031, *Golden Plover*. Note the tidy condition of this area of the shed.

J. S. Everitt

74 Perth shed on 5th June 1965 presents an untidy appearance in contrast to the previous photograph. Various axle-box springs litter the yard, with piles of brake blocks and rocking-grate bars. Nearly all the engines visible in this picture are of LMSR origin, except Class A4 No. 60031, *Golden Plover*, which spent some time out of use during the summer of 1965. It was noted lying at Cowlairs Works at the end of July with its motion disconnected, but returned to service the following month. It even managed a stint on the three-hour trains, working the 8.25am Buchanan Street-Aberdeen and 5.15pm return on the 25th/26th August. Its reliability was doubtful however, and it was taken off the 8.25am from Glasgow at Perth on 27th August. It again returned to traffic, but was finally withdrawn in October 1965 and subsequently scrapped.

Martin S. Welch

5 Perth motive power depot's massive coaling plant dominated the immediate surrounding area, doubtless much to the annoyance of local residents, unless of course one of the family worked on the railway! In this view, taken from the eastern side of the main line, a Class 5, No. 44795, is seen passing the shed in charge of the 10.35am Glasgow to Inverness train on 21st August 1965. The steam engine was presumably due to be replaced by a diesel on arrival at Perth. Note the line of stored locomotives in a siding opposite the depot. On this date the preserved Highland Railway 'Jones Goods' 4-6-0 No. 103 journeyed from Perth to Inverness in connection with the centenary of the Highland Railway and can just be discerned, together with one of the two Caledonian Railway coaches which formed its train, stabled on one of the far sidings. *D. Hume*

76 This 1951 view from St. Leonards Bridge depicts an unidentified ex-CR 4-4-0 approaching the station, which in those far-off days was known as Perth General. The signal box, which took its name from the adjoining bridge, was one of many in the Perth area closed in the early 1960s when a new colour-light signalling scheme was introduced, thus rendering redundant the ancient semaphore equipment seen here. The former NBR locomotive shed, the shadow of which is just visible, occupied a site immediately opposite the signal box. *P. Hay*

St Leonards bridge, located immediately south of Perth station's platforms offers a superb vantage point from where to observe trains approaching from the south, and also those waiting departure from the station. In the mid-1960s the author recalls a convenient flight of steps which connected the up main platform with the bridge, thus enabling an energetic enthusiast to photograph an incoming northbound train and then race down the steps onto the station to obtain a second picture of it leaving! There was also a handily-placed fish and chip shop adjoining the bridge, while for those requiring sustenance when that establishment was closed, the station's staff canteen offered basic fare to those not requiring Egon Ronay standards. Certainly, in those days it seems everything possible was laid on to provide for the visiting steam enthusiasts. Sadly, the steps have now disappeared, while the staff canteen has doubtless shared the same fate. Perhaps the chip shop survives despite a dramatic drop in turnover since September 1966!

77 Fifteen years later, on 30th August 1966, No. 60019, *Bittern,* slows for its Perth stop with the six-coach 5.30pm Glasgow to Aberdeen train. The semaphore signals have gone, the track layout has been simplified and the (then) relatively-new power box stands on the site of the old NBR engine shed adjacent to the goods lines. The line of trees in the middle background and distant hills, however, continue to provide a distinctive setting.
D. E. Gouldthorp

Perth

78 On the first day of the new three-hour service, 18th June 1962, Class A4 No. 60011, *Empire of India*, leaves Perth with the 7.10am from Aberdeen. The photographer recalls that the train left sixteen minutes late, at 9.7am, due to the locomotive being detached to take water. Somewhat unusually, the train had been routed into the down main platform which of course did not have a water column at the southern end. When colour-light signalling was introduced the opportunity was taken to establish reversible working on most lines in the station area to give greater flexibility, but obviously the requirements of steam traction had not been fully taken into account!   *W. A. C. Smith*

79 Taking water presents no problem for No. 60532, *Blue Peter,* as it awaits departure with the 1.30pm Aberdeen to Glasgow train on 18th July 1966. It is standing at Perth station's 1,672 feet long up main platform.   *D. Hume*

80 The 8.29am Dundee Tay Bridge to Perth empty coaching stock train waits at Perth's curving up Dundee line platform on 2nd July 1966 with Class B1 4-6-0 No. 61263 in charge. This working was usually powered by a Class B1, V2 or A2 Pacific from Tay Bridge depot.   *D. Hume*

81 On 6th September 1951, a former CR 4-4-0 No. 54499 lays a smoke screen across the south end of the station as it departs on unidentified working. Note the extremely dilapidated condition of the station buildings. *P. H.*

The first railway to reach Perth was the line from Dundee: this was opened on 24th May 1847 by the Dundee and Per Railway. It did not, however, enter the city but terminated on the east bank of the River Tay, at Barnhill. Bridging of t river was completed within two years, thus enabling trains from Dundee to make connection with those from the sou Initially a timber bridge across the river was constructed, but this proved unsatisfactory and was soon replaced by a sto structure. The second railway to reach Perth was the SCR, which inaugurated a service from Larbert, Stirling, Gleneagles a Auchterarder in May 1848. Within a few months the CR's extension to Greenhill made through running all the way London a reality. Another route from the south reached the southern outskirts of Perth at the same time. This was t Edinburgh and Northern Railway's line from Ladybank which joined up with the Scottish Central at Hilton Junction. provided a shorter route to Edinburgh using the Burntisland ferry. This line lost its local passenger service in Septemb 1955, but following the closure of the principal Edinburgh – Perth line via Glenfarg in 1970 was granted a new lease of life a through route between the two cities. Returning to the original development of railways at Perth, the next line to enter t city, in August 1848, was the Scottish Midland Junction Railway's (SMJR) line from Forfar. No fewer than three other lin met the Forfar route within a few miles of Perth. The branch to Dunkeld, which later became part of the Highland main lir was opened in April 1856 while the Perth, Almond Valley and Methven Railway opened the first section of its line – betwe Perth and Methven Junction – in 1858. This company was quickly taken over by the CR which continued the line on Crieff and eventually a junction with the Dunblane – Oban line at Balquhidder. The last section was not, however, open until 1905 and closed in 1951, so one wonders if its construction was worth the effort! The third line to join up with t SMJR's line was the short branch from Strathord to Bankfoot, which was very late on the scene, opening in 1906, and losi its passenger service as early as 1931; freight traffic lingered on to the mid-1960s.

In 1863, when the railways in the city were developing rapidly the Perth General Station Joint committee w established. This body was constituted by representatives of the various railways using the station, but within three years series of amalgamations had reduced the number of companies using Perth General to just three – the Caledonian, the No British and the Highland. The first mentioned naturally had by far the greatest number of representatives on the board, t North British having only two and the Highland just one. Following the 1923 amalgamation the newly-formed LMSR becar the principal owners of the station, the LNER having only two representatives on the committee.

2 You can almost feel the cold as No. 60034, *Lord Faringdon,* poses for its picture on a freezing night at Perth in early 1966. The ocomotive was in the course of working the 11.2pm from Glasgow to Aberdeen, and was presumably engaged in some shunting work before resuming its journey north. This train was due in the Granite City at around 3.20am, giving Class A4 devotees a wait of just under our hours until the 7.10am to Glasgow was due to leave. Alternatively, for the less patient enthusiast there was always the 6.20am to erth!

M. S. Burns

3 'Britannia' Pacific No. 70031, formerly amed *Byron,* blows off impatiently as it aits for the road. The train is an afternoon outhbound fish working from Aberdeen, and e date is 8th June 1965.

J. S. Whiteley

84 The up afternoon travelling post office train (Postal) from Aberdeen stands beneath Perth station's grime-encrusted overall roof on 20 April 1965. Motive power is provided by No. 60006, *Sir Ralph Wedgwood.* The tracks on the right lead to the carriage shed. No. 6000 was built at Doncaster works in 1938 as No. 4466, *Herring Gull.* In January 1944 the machine was renamed *Sir Ralph Wedgwood,* th nameplates being transferred from a sister engine which was damaged beyond repair during an air raid at York on 29th April 1942. N 60006 was a resident of Kings Cross Top Shed for most of its working life – being officially transferred to Scotland in October 1963. spent seven months in store at Dalry Road shed, Edinburgh, before joining Ferryhill's stud of Pacifics on 4th May 1964. It lasted almo another eighteen months in service before withdrawal in September 1965 and met its end at the Motherwell Machinery and Scra Company's Wishaw yard later the same year.

J. S. Whitele

85 The wind gathers the exhaust of Class A4 No. 60019, *Bittern,* into a magnificent column as it leaves Perth hauling the 5.30p Glasgow to Aberdeen on 30th August 1966, during the final week of regular A4 operation. The 7.10am Aberdeen to Glasgow ar 5.30pm return had been regularly diesel worked for some months and the reappearance of *Bittern* was a delightful surprise. These trains we also worked by *Bittern* the following day. No. 60024, *Kingfisher,* was the only other A4 operational by this date, and it worked th 1.30pm *ex*-Aberdeen on Monday 29th August, but was replaced by *Blue Peter* for the following four days. After working the same train c Friday 2nd September *Blue Peter* was sent to Edinburgh to work a rail tour to Aberdeen the next day, the 1.30pm being worked by Class No. 44703 on the Saturday.

D. E. Gouldthor

86 In the days before the introduction of colour-light signals at Perth, Class V2 No. 60827 leaves with the 5.30pm Glasgow – Aberdeen on 21st June 1957. This was the return locomotive working of the 3.30pm Aberdeen to Perth 'Postal'. Note the amazing selection of vehicles marshalled immediately behind the locomotive, one of which appears to be a milk tank wagon. The two tracks on the right are the goods lines which avoided the main station area.

J. L. Stevenson

Northbound from Perth

87 Yes, another picture of *Bittern,* but who could possibly resist including this gem of a photograph of No. 60019 leaving Perth with the 5.30pm from Glasgow on 15th July 1965? *S. C. Nash*

88 On 3rd September 1960, a Pickersgill Class 3P Caley Bogie 4-4-0, No. 54485, passes Balhousie signal box on its way out of Perth with the 3.42pm train to Blair Atholl, on the Highland main line to Inverness. There were forty-eight engines of this type which lasted in traffic until December 1962, a number being employed towards the end on passenger trains on the Highland section. No. 54485 achieved fame when it featured, together with sister locomotive No. 54486, on a BBC 'Railway Roundabout' television programme. The pair of veterans were specially rostered to work a train over the Perth to Aviemore Highland route.

D. Hume

89 Two passenger coaches and a couple of vans hardly constitute a taxing assignment for No. 60024 *Kingfisher,* as it hauls the 6.30am Perth to Aberdeen local train near Luncarty, just north of Perth, on 2nd August 1966. Interestingly, very few pictures of the Perth to Aberdeen local trains were submitted for publication: presumably most photographers did not consider them worth the effort. One wonders if there are any illustrations available of a Class A4 Pacific hauling a shorter passenger train than this!

J. Dagley-Morris

90 In the 1960s the curiously-named town of Coupar Angus, almost sixteen miles north of Perth, was the only one between Perth and Forfar to retain a train service. The other towns such as Blairgowrie and Alyth lost their passenger services in the preceding decade. This picture shows Coupar Angus station on 27th August 1960 with Class A2 No. 60528, *Tudor Minstrel,* entering in charge of the 9.30am Aberdeen to Glasgow train. Oddly, Coupar Angus is not located in the county of Angus, as the name suggests, but in Perthshire. The section of line from Stanley Junction to Forfar did not close completely until 1982, and ten years later rails embedded in a main road, level crossing gates and the shell of a signal box still offered tangible reminders of the railway's existence.

D. Hume

Coupar Angus

91 The 9.30am Aberdeen to Glasgow train is seen again, but this time on 24th August 1963, and with different motive power. The locomotive in charge is No. 60041, *Salmon Trout,* which had been disfigured by German-type smoke deflectors. No. 60041 was originally constructed at Doncaster in late 1934 and survived in service until December 1965, when it was the penultimate Class A3 in traffic.

D. Hume

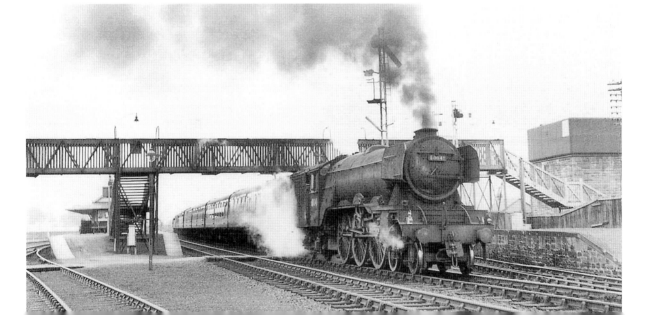

92 Alyth Junction station was probably the most interesting country junction on the line, at one time being served by trains from Dundee via Newtyle, which crossed the main line on a bridge west of the station, and then dropped rapidly to enter their own platform on the north side of the station. The short branch line to Alyth, just over five miles away, met the main line here, as the station's name implies. Trains from Dundee were able to proceed directly to Alyth, but had to reverse to reach the main line tracks. In this illustration former CR 0-6-0 No. 57581 is depicted waiting in the Newtyle platform with a rail tour in June 1962. The Sidlaw Hills form the background, together with a cluster of buildings around the station. *D. Hume*

Alyth Junction

93 On 14th August 1954, a former CR 0-4-4T locomotive, No. 55169, stands in the down platform at Alyth Junction with the 11.28am (SO) Dundee West to Blairgowrie train, after reversing and running round. This station probably offered everything the railway lover could wish for – a most unusual layout, fascinating train working and signalling, and, of course, not too many passengers milling about to distract him from his observations!

P. Hay

94 Class A4 Pacific No. 60016, *Silver King,* passes through the western outskirts of Forfar with the 3.30pm mails and passenger train from Aberdeen on 4th July 1964. No. 60016, built in 1935, was stationed at Gateshead for the greater part of its life, moving to Scotland in the autumn of 1963. It was withdrawn for scrap in March, 1965. *M. Mensing*

95 In wintry conditions, an unidentified train for Glasgow leaves Forfar on 4th February 1961 behind Aberdeen Ferryhill-allocated Class A2 Pacific No. 60531, *Bahram.* *W. S. Sellar*

Forfar

The first railway to reach Forfar was the 5ft 6in gauge line from Arbroath, on which a service commenced on 4th Decemb[er] 1838, using horse power! This arrangement did not last long, however, locomotives taking over a month later. The origin[al] terminus station was at Play Field just south of the spot where the town's main station was later constructed. This line w[as] built primarily for freight traffic, particularly coal from the docks at Arbroath, which was distributed to the towns [of] Strathmore, and stone which was despatched to English ports from the local quarries in the Sidlaw Hills. Just under ten yea[rs] later the Perth to Forfar line was opened by the Scottish Midland Junction Railway, so by this time the townsfolk were able [to] reach every major settlement in the area by rail, although it was some years before a direct service to Dundee was provide[d.] The final line built in the area, was the fifteen miles-long branch from Forfar to Brechin, opened in 1895 which traversed [a] very thinly-populated agricultural area. This was reflected in the sparse train service provided which, in the summer 195[?] timetable, consisted of only two return trains on weekdays only. Not surprisingly this tranquil backwater was closed [to] passenger traffic the following year. Sadly, the next fifteen years witnessed a series of passenger service closures, culminatin[g] in the withdrawal of services along the Strathmore route in September 1967. Freight traffic along the Stanley Junctio[n–] Forfar section continued until June 1982.

97 A former NBR Class D30, No. 62427, *Dumbiedykes,* awaits departure from Forfar with the 2.58pm train to Arbroath on 27th January 1952. This working will use the metals of the main Strathmore route until it branches off just after Guthrie, seven miles fro[m] Forfar, and turns south eventually to join the former NBR Arbroath to Montrose line at St. Vigean's Junction, a mile or so from Arbroat[h.] The route closed in 1955, by which time it had become the last surviving branch line to operate from Forfar.   *J. L. Stevenso[n]*

8 A shunter looks on as *ex-CR 0-6-0 No.* 57441 carries out some light shunting work across a street in Forfar on 25th February 1961. This short goods branch occupied the route of the original broad gauge (5ft. 6ins.) line from Arbroath opened in 1838. A short section of this branch near the town centre ran on an embankment, which was still clearly visible in 1991.   *W. A. C. Smith*

9 Forfar shed was opened on 18th December 1899 and replaced another built many years earlier. The 'new' shed was constructed on bare ground to the north of the station and was a quite attractive building, built of brick. A coaling stage was provided on the north side of the yards, and a 54-feet diameter turntable was also part of the depot's facilities. Forfar shed's allocation usually hovered around twenty locomotives, nearly all of CR origin, although three LMSR Hughes 'Mogul' 2-6-0s were allocated there for a time. The locomotives were employed on a variety of mundane tasks, hauling local passenger and goods trains to Dundee, Arbroath, Brechin, Alyth and Kirriemuir. The closure of some local lines in the 1950s caused a gradual reduction in Forfar's complement and in 1959 the shed was reduced in status to a sub-shed of Perth. Final closure came in July 1964. In this view former CR 4-4-0 No. 54467, complete with a snowplough, is depicted standing outside the shed on 2nd August 1959.   *D. Hume*

100 One of the saddest experiences for a railway lover is to visit a place that was once prominent on the railway map, but has since lost all rail connection. Brecon, Woodford Halse and Melton Constable immediately spring to mind, but few people would think of Forfar, which was the principal railway centre on the Strathmore route. In days gone by six routes were operationally centred on Forfar, the main line connecting with Perth and Aberdeen, and local branches which served Arbroath, Brechin, Kirriemuir and Dundee. The rot set in in the early 1950s when the Brechin and Kirriemuir branches – both of which had a very sparse service – were shut in August 1952. Fifteen years later, in September 1967, the Strathmore route itself fell victim to Doctor Beeching's axe, and after another fifteen year period the Forfar to Stanley Junction section, which had been retained for freight purposes, was also closed thus removing Forfar from the railway map. When this picture of No. 54500 arriving with the daily freight from Careston, on the truncated Brechin line, was taken on 29th July 1961 Forfar still seems to be a reasonably busy centre. At the time of writing the engine shed – which is used by a car repair firm – still stands as a reminder of the past, but everything else of railway interest in this picture has gone for ever.

D. Hume

01 A rail tour, hauled by *ex*-CR 0-6-0 No. 57581, passes Forfar North Junction signal box on 17th June 1962. Note the lifted tracks of the line to Dundee on the right. The two coaches immediately behind the locomotive are the preserved CR vehicles which were often used on trains of this type.

D. Hume

02 In the author's opinion the age of steam was rarely as romantic or glamorous as sometimes portrayed. Certainly, for footplate and shed staff, working with steam on an everyday basis was often dirty and laborious. Who would envy the footplatemen of No. 54489, seen here waiting to leave Forfar with the daily Careston goods, on a bitterly cold day in February 1961? The primitive footplate conditions on the outward journey would doubtless be uncomfortable enough, then they would have returned tender first, presumably with only a storm sheet for protection. There must have been easier ways of earning a living!

W. S. Sellar

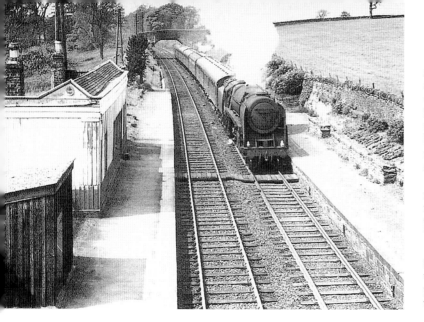

103 The little-known, and presumably little photographed station of Auldbar Road was situated five miles east of Forfar adjacent to the attractive Balgavies Loch. The author has been unable to establish how the station acquired its name, there being no settlement in the vicinity named 'Auldbar', though there is a reference to 'Aldbar'. Perhaps all this is academic because the station only served a few local farms and even in the early 1950s had a poor service; most of the trains that did stop were Forfar to Arbroath 'locals'. The station closed on 11th June 1956, but in this picture it still seems to be reasonably intact. Balgavies Loch is just out of sight behind the trees on the left. The train is an Abington, near Carstairs to Aberdeen schools special hauled by 'Britannia' Pacific No. 70016, *Ariel,* and the photograph was taken on 30th May 1966. When the author visited the site in 1991 nature was rapidly taking over the former station area, but the platforms were clearly visible. The road overbridge, from where this picture was taken, remains, likewise the old signal box (not visible in the picture) now used as a greenhouse.   *D. Hume*

Auldbar Road

104 On 5th August 1965, Class A4 No. 60007, *Sir Nigel Gresley,* passes Auldbar Road in charge of a Glasgow-bound express.   *J. Dagley-Morris*

05 The 1.30pm Aberdeen to Glasgow train, hauled by Class 5 No. 44794, passes the site of Farnell Road station on 28th May 1966. The locomotive is working hard at this point as the train has just started the four miles-long climb of Farnell Road bank, the gradients of which vary from 1 in 100 at the foot, to 1 in 143 just before the summit at the approach to the former Glasterlaw station. Farnell Road was another of the isolated wayside stations which closed in the mid-1950s. The 1951 summer timetable reveals that this station was only served by two trains in each direction on weekdays, but at least this meagre service was better than that of Glasterlaw, which had been closed in April of that year.

D. Hume

06 Class A4 No. 60024, *Kingfisher*, wheels the 1.30pm *ex*-Aberdeen along the level section of line between Bridge of Dun and Farnell Road on 25th August 1966.

I. S. Krause

107 On 12th April 1966, No 60024, *Kingfisher,* crosses the River South Esk, west of Bridge of Dun, with the 1.30pm Aberdeen to Glasgow train.

C. E. Weston

Bridge of Dun

108 'The Grampian', the 1.30pm from Aberdeen to Glasgow, is seen again as inappropriately named Class A2 No. 60527, *Sun Chariot,* re-starts from Bridge of Dun on the wet afternoon of 7th September 1963. This station is now maintained by the Brechin Railway Preservation Society who have assembled an impressive collection of rolling stock. Steam trains are occasionally operated along the line to Brechin, which the society eventually hopes to re-open as a tourist railway.
W. A. C. Smith

109 A local freight train from Montrose to Brechin enters Bridge of Dun station on 18th July 1966, behind Class J37 No. 64620. Note the very substantially-built water tank on the left of the picture.
J. G. Mallinson

10 Smoke by arrangement! The crew of Class V2 2-6-2 No. 60919 provide a splendid smoke effect for the photographer as they depart ɔm Bridge of Dun with a Perth to Aberdeen stopping train in 1966. In June of that year this machine made the long trek to the former ɔuthern Region to work a rail tour from Waterloo, but suffered a mechanical failure and was unable to fulfil its assignment, on which a ɪlleid Light Pacific was substituted.
M. S. Burns

111 The 7.10am Aberdeen to Glasgow train approaches Bridge of Dun on 5th August 1965. Motive power is provided by No. 60009, *Union of South Africa*, which was probably the longest serving of all the Class A4s on this route. *John Goss*

112 At Dubton Junction station, a short branch line diverged in a south-eastern direction to Montrose. The station was adjacent to the village of Hillside, but there was little local traffic and in the summer 1951 timetable a total of only eight main line trains was booked to call. Passengers from Montrose were provided with reasonable connections on to westbound trains, but in the opposite direction the connections were generally made at Bridge of Dun. The station closed on 4th August 1952, the day on which passenger services between Montrose and Brechin were withdrawn. In this picture former CR 0-6-0 No. 57324 is seen pausing at Dubton Junction with the 2.0pm Montrose to Brechin train on 28th October 1950. It is presumably providing a connection on to the 1.15pm Aberdeen to Glasgow train, two vehicles of which can be seen at the adjoining platform. *J. L. Stevenson*

13 Class 5 4-6-0 No. 44982 passes the remains of Dubton Junction station with the 9.0am freight train from Perth to Aberdeen on 28th May 1966.
D. Hume

14 The famous Kinnaber Junction signal box is just visible towards the rear of the train as Class A2 Pacific No. 60532, *Blue Peter*, rounds the curve with a southbound train during the summer of 1966.
John Goss

115 On 18th May 1966, Class J37 No. 64602 has just left Bridge of Dun station, and is proceeding towards Brechin with the daily freight from Montrose. The rich soil in this area makes it good farming country, and much agricultural traffic was carried on the railway, particularly seed potatoes during the season. *W. A. C. Smith*

Brechin Branch

It is unfortunate that the city of Brechin, one of the largest settlements in the area and a commercial centre serving a sizeable rural hinterland, never had a main line railway service. It was a victim of railway building 'politics' of the 1840 and condemned to a lowly status at the end of a branch line from Bridge of Dun, while the principal route in the area passed by a mere three miles to the south! If the original promoters of the main Perth – Forfar – Aberdeen line had taken a less direct route and attempted to serve some of the small towns in the area (such as Brechin, Blairgowrie and Kirriemuir) the line might have escaped closure in 1967. Brechin's fate was decided in 1844 when, initially at least, it seemed that the city would be served directly by the Aberdeen Railway's proposed line which was routed via Stonehaven Laurencekirk, and Brechin before connecting with the Arbroath and Forfar line at Guthrie. The appointment of a consulting engineer, William Cubitt, resulted in friction between the Aberdeen Railway and the Scottish Midland Junction Railway, with which the line via Brechin had been agreed. Cubitt approved the Aberdeen Railway's route only as far as Laurencekirk, from where the proposed line deviated from that previously agreed, by-passing Brechin by a few miles to the south-east. When the citizens of Brechin heard of the change of plan they, and the Scottish Midland Junction Railway, were furious, so much so that the latter proposed another railway, from near Forfar to Marykirk (north of Montrose) in order to serve Brechin. This proposal was thrown out by Parliament, however, while the Aberdeen Railway's plans were accepted. So Brechin's position at the end of a short branch was confirmed. The three-and-a-half miles-long branch was opened on 1st February 1848 to the accompaniment of much celebration and rejoicing. The inaugural train ran from Montrose to Brechin (and other locations) conveying invited guests and local dignitaries: it took twenty-five minutes to cover the ten-and-a-half miles which separated the towns. Two other lines served Brechin, one the route to Forfar and the other the branch to Edzell, which ran more or less due north from Brechin. There was one intermediate station at Stracathro (formerly Inchbare). This route, like that to Forfar, served a thinly inhabited area, and lost its passenger service in 1931. Perhaps the line's only claim to fame is the fact that the passenger trains were reinstated for a brief three month period during the summer of 1938. The line closed completely in 1964 when the last goods train ran.

116 Another view of a freight from Montrose, this time No. 64576 provides the motive power and the train is seen approaching Brechin on 25th August 1966.
I. S. Krause

117 A few weeks prior to closure to passenger traffic 'Compound' 4-4-0 No. 40939 is pictured leaving Brechin at the head of an excursion to Guthrie, on 12th July 1952. No. 40939 is believed to have been the sole member of its class allocated to Forfar shed at this time. Brechin station is just out of sight beyond the road bridge on the extreme left of the picture. Note the line to Edzell and Forfar, via Careston, climbing steeply on the right behind the telegraph pole.
J. L. Stevenson

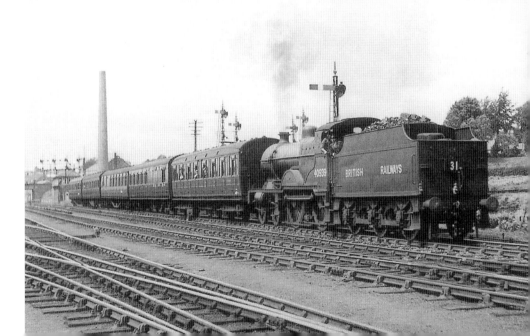

118 A general view of the semi-derelict station and goods yard at Brechin on 12th May 1966, with Class J37 No. 64602 carrying out some shunting.

J. J. Smith

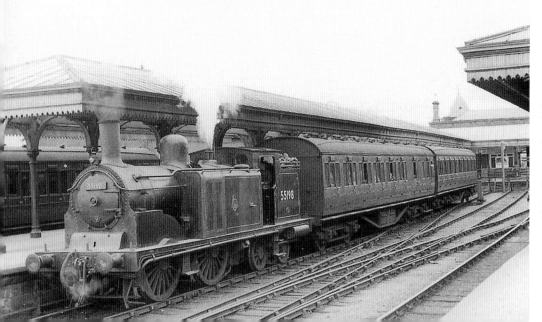

119 Former CR 0-4-4T locomotive No. 55198 blows off impatiently prior to departure from Brechin with the 2.5pm to Forfar via Careston on 12th July 1952. This line, which served a few scattered rural communities, closed to passengers a few weeks later. The fifteen miles-long journey took twenty-five minutes. *J. L. Stevenson*

120 A local freight enters Brechin behind *ex*-CR 0-4-4T locomotive No. 55185 on 12th July 1952. *J. L. Stevenson*

21 The 1.25pm freight from Montrose poses at Brechin station on 5th August 1965.

J. Dagley-Morris

122 Mention Princes Street station to the average railway enthusiast and he will automatically think of the former C Edinburgh terminus which was closed in September, 1965. There was, however another station with the same name at Perth, located just half a mile along the Dundee line between the main station (which was previously known as 'Perth General') and the bridge across the River Tay. Perth Princes Street station was within a single line section which extended to Barnhill signal box, on the opposite bank of the river. In this picture, taken on the 16th August 1958, a Fairburn designed LMSR 2-6-4T locomotive, No. 42691, pauses at Princes Street station while working the 5.25pm Dundee West Perth. This station was shut on 28th February 1966, thus outlasting its Edinburgh namesake by five months.

D. Hume

123 Kinnoull Hill, which rises to a height of 728 feet above sea level, provides the backdrop to this study of Class A2 Pacific No. 60530 *Sayajirao* on the 10.0am Dundee to Glasgow in August 1965. The author is unaware of the reason for the appearance of this locomotive on this train on at least two occasions at this time, but has heard two suggestions put forward. One is simply that an enthusiast altered the roster board at Tay Bridge shed, while another is that the Scottish Region turned out No. 60530 as a favour for an enthusiast who had supplied publicity photographs. What more impressive publicity picture could there be than *Sayajirao* hauling a rake of maroon coaches, as seen here? The stone viaduct in the middle of the scene was built on Moncrieffe Island which is an interesting feature at this point.

J. G. Mallinson

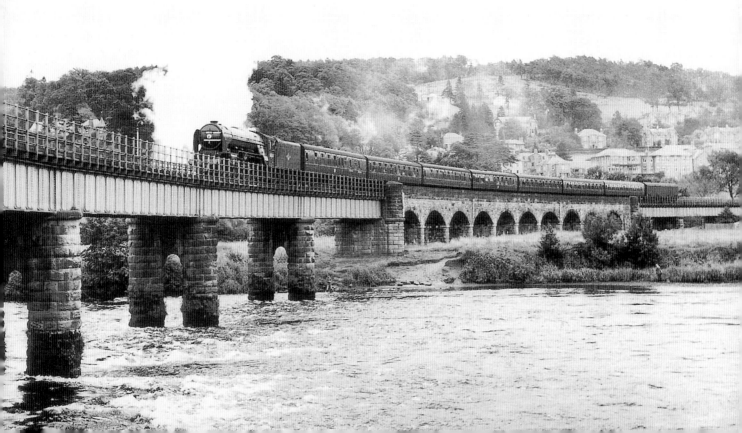

124 The 9.15am from Glasgow to Dundee, hauled by No. 60031, *Golden Plover,* curves round towards Barnhill signal box on 27th August 1964. The grimy condition of No. 60031 will be noted; presumably engine cleaners at St. Rollox shed were in short supply at this time. In 1962 a resignalling scheme was completed at Perth, but its scope was limited compared with current schemes when hundreds of track miles can be easily controlled by one power box. Barnhill box was unaffected by the resignalling and remains in use at the time of writing.

P. S. Leavens

The twenty-one miles-long section of line from Perth to Dundee takes passengers across the fertile plain of the Carse of Gowrie. The line is bordered on one side by the southern slopes of the Sidlaw Hills and on the other by the Firth of Tay. Originally the gauge of the line was intended to be 5ft 6in in common with some other railways in the area, but for once common sense prevailed and the line's promoters, the Dundee & Perth Railway, adopted the 4ft 8½ in gauge which was starting to be commonly accepted as standard further south. Apart from the viaduct which carries the line across the city for three quarters of a mile to the former Perth Princes Street station, and the bridge spanning the River Tay, there are few engineering works of note. Gradients are hardly noticeable and there are long sections of level track. One point of interest concerns the long-defunct Inchture tramway, opened in 1848 to connect the station with the village, two miles away. Until 1895 an old horse-drawn composite railway coach was employed, but during that year a specially-constructed vehicle, similar to a single deck tramcar – painted in Caledonian Railway colours – took over. The service remained in operation until 1916 when it was withdrawn as a war-time economy measure and never reinstated. By that time, it was the last horse-drawn tram service on the British mainland. In 1849 a similar branch was provided between Errol Station and village but was uneconomic and closed after three years' operation.

125 The 8.29am Dundee to Perth empty stock train approaches Barnhill behind Class V2 No. 60919 on 18th July 1966.

J. G. Mallinson

126 Photographed on the same day as the previous picture No. 60919 steams across a bridge over a flooded quarr at Invergowrie with the 8.29am from Dundee. This machine was one of the last Class V2 locomotives in service, an the author will never forget a rousing run behind it when hauling the 6.0pm SuO Aberdeen to Glasgow train as far a Dundee, on a dismal August evening in 1965. The three cylinder exhaust beat was a joy to hear, the engine having t be worked almost to its limit with the heavy train. No. 60919 was built at Darlington in 1941 and saw service briefly a Heaton, Gateshead and Tweedmouth depots in north east England before migrating to Aberdeen Ferryhill shed i 1945. It remained there for almost twenty years, until November 1964, when it moved to Dundee Tay Bridge shed. was withdrawn six weeks after this view was taken, and subsequently sold for breaking-up at Arnott Young's yard, Ol Kilpatrick.

C. E. Westor

127 Shortly before Dundee Tay Bridge station is reached a junction is made with the line from Edinburgh which drops down from the Tay Bridge. In this view Class A3 Pacific No. 60099, *Call Boy,* is seen alongside Tay Bridge shed yard which is on the right of the picture. It was working the 10.2am Millerhill to Dundee freight on 21st September 1963. The locomotive is fitted with hideous German-type smoke deflectors which, in the author's opinion, completely ruined the appearance of these otherwise handsome machines.

W. S. Sellar

128 A former NBR Class J37 0-6-0, No. 64620, carries out mundane shunting duties at Tay Bridge goods and mineral sidings on 27th August 1964. This locomotive type was a very common sight in this area for decades and by 1964 almost a third of the remaining members of the class were allocated to Tay Bridge shed for local freight duties. The tracks to the left of the J37 are the main running lines and beyond them the shed building.

P. S. Leavens

Tay Bridge Shed by day . . .

129 In characteristic pose Tay Bridge motive power depot's two stand-b[y] locomotives – Nos. 60530, *Sayajirao,* and 60532, *Blue Peter* – awa[it] their next calls of duty on 28th May 1966. Enthusiasts visiting Scotland a[t] this time were often frustrated by the sight of these magnificent machine[s] simply sitting on shed in steam, usually looking as though they were abou[t] to move off at any minute. Their workings were always unpredictable, bu[t] at least when *Blue Peter* moved to Ferryhill shed, for use on the Glasgo[w] trains a few weeks after this picture was taken, steam fans were given [a] final opportunity to photograph the class on express passenger work[.] Sister engine No. 60528, *Tudor Minstrel,* also based at Dundee at th[is] time, was equally elusive on line work.   *Martin S. Welc[h]*

. . . and by night

130 Class A2 No. 60532, *Blue Peter,* simmers gently at Dundee Ta[y] Bridge shed on the night of 29th August 1965.   *D. E. Gouldthorp[e]*

Dundee Tay
Bridge Station

131 Class B1 4-6-0 No. 61180, of Tay Bridge shed, makes an energetic ascent of the stiff 1 in 66 climb away from Tay Bridge station's down platform hauling a short train of empty stock bound for Thornton Junction, on 7th August 1965. It is in the process of crossing to the up line. In the author's view, despite light and airy facilities at street level, this is the drabbest main line station in Scotland. Note the station was partially surrounded by goods yards on both sides. *D. Hume*

132 Class V2 2-6-2 No. 60813 was the only example of its class to be fitted with a stovepipe chimney and small semi-circular smoke deflector. This picture gives an excellent view of this rather curious feature. No. 60813 was to become one of the last V2s to remain in service, not being withdrawn until September 1966. The dingy location of Tay Bridge station's platforms will be noted. The train in view is the 8.35am Aberdeen to London Kings Cross, and the photograph was taken on 14th August 1960. *D. Hume*

133 Passing a pair of unusual signal brackets with bi-directional arms, Class 5 No. 45184 makes a brisk start away from Dundee West powering the 10.0am Glasgow train on a snowy 28th December 1964. *D. Hume*

Dundee West

134 Dundee West, the CR's terminus in the city, was opened in 1889 with a fine frontage on to South Union Street. It was by far the most impressive of the city's three stations and had an agreeably spacious air. It had four platform faces, with platform Nos. 2 and 3 being the longest, each accommodating eleven coaches plus an engine. The other platforms were shorter bays and were each able to hold eight carriages and a locomotive. Unfortunately, in addition to being the city's most attractive station, it was also the quietest and by the late 1950s, after withdrawal of the Newtyle branch trains in January 1955, was handling only sixteen trains each way daily. These consisted of seven expresses to Glasgow and nine local trains to Perth, but the latter only had three wayside stations to serve by this time, most of the smaller stations having already fallen under the axe in June 1956. Here, one of St. Rollox depot's Caprotti-fitted Standard Class 5s, No. 73146, waits to leave Dundee West with the 2.0pm departure to Glasgow on 27th April 1963. Dundee West station was closed in May 1965. *D. Hume*

135 Looking at this view of former CR 0-4-4T locomotive No. 55217 leaving Dundee West on a one-coach train to Blairgowrie on 16th September 1950, it is not difficult to see why the line closed. Perhaps, judging by the total lack of any visible passengers, one should wonder how it remained in business for so long! However, the run over the Sidlaw Hills to Newtyle, followed by a quick sprint along the former CR main line to Coupar Angus, before branching off to Blairgowrie, must have been an absolutely fascinating trip. The service provided at this time was most peculiar, with the timetable advertising five trains each way from Dundee to Blairgowrie. Three of these ran only on Saturdays, however, and the first Monday to Friday service from Dundee was not until 4.20pm followed by another train at 5.40pm. In the reverse direction there were two morning trains to Dundee, so it would appear that the service was run principally for workpeople, with no other trains on offer, except on Saturdays!
J. L. Stevenson

ndee is, of course, famous for the 3,509 yards-long Tay Bridge, but less widely known is the fact that one of Scotland's rliest railways had a terminus in the city. This was the Dundee & Newtyle which was authorised in 1826 and opened in 331. It was purely a local line built without any reference to the embryonic national system. For the first thirty years of peration the railway used a variety of haulage systems employing two locomotives, three stationary steam engines to work clines, and a horse. Not bad for an eleven miles-long line! Unfortunately the railway was in dire financial difficulties right om the start and it was not until the late 1860s, when various diversions were constructed around the railway's three clines, the steepest of which was 1 in 10, that the line was operated by more orthodox means. The route closed to ssengers in January 1955 and was later shut to freight traffic, the track being subsequently lifted. The course of the line is ll visible for a considerable distance, and the original station building plus a turntable pit still survive at Newtyle. Another ite early scheme, this time serving the eastern fringe of the city, was proposed in 1836. This was the Dundee & Arbroath ilway which was the brainchild of Lord Panmure, a local landowner, through whose land most of the line passed. The lack any major engineering works meant that the line was swiftly constructed and it opened for business on 6th October 1838. e most remarkable point about this line was probably the gauge of 5ft 6in. adopted on the advice of the well known gineer, Thomas Grainger, who considered the 'standard' (4ft 8½in) gauge too narrow. The line's first Dundee terminus as situated on the outskirts of the city at Craigie, but the track was soon extended to a more convenient terminus at Trades ne which opened on 2nd April 1840. This station was constructed by the Dundee Harbour Trustees who controlled the ilway within the harbour area under the terms of the original Act. The railway soon realised it was way out of step with her concerns and altered its gauge in 1847. In December 1857 a new station, Dundee East, opened immediately to the rth of Trades Lane station, which was then closed.

Meanwhile, on the western side of the city the line to Perth had been in operation since 1847 from a station roughly on e site of Dundee West. Trains from Newtyle used their own station at Ward Road until the opening of a new deviation ilway and junction with the Perth line at Ninewells diverted trains into Dundee West in June 1861. Interchange of traffic tween the two railways was effected by horse-haulage over a street railway half a mile in length which connected the two stems. A scheme to construct a viaduct across the town to link the separate railways had been suggested in 1848 but came nothing, so for more than thirty years the tramway was the only connection between them. This situation came to an end 1878, however, when the NBR reached the city from Fife via the Tay Bridge, and constructed their Tay Bridge station. is was constructed in a dingy, narrow cutting below high-water level and it seems odd that after approaching the city at a gh level the NBR should choose to drop their line down in such a way as to necessitate a 1 in 66 climb up to Camperdown nction on the eastern exit from the station. The opening of the Tay Bridge transformed rail communications to the city and ernight the Dundee – Arbroath section, previously purely a local line, became part of a through route to Aberdeen.

136 Dundee East, the Dundee and Arbroath Joint station, was a smaller version of the CR's West station, but its traffic was much more localised in character. The station, built alongside the East Coast main line as it climbs out of Dock Street tunnel, generally offered a service of around a dozen trains on weekdays to Arbroath plus a few short workings at peak hours to Carnoustie. In the late 1950s these services were largely the preserve of a small fleet of Class C16 4-4-2T locomotives based at Tay Bridge shed. One of these machines, No. 67502, built for the NBR in 1915, stands in the East station on 8th October 1958. At one time a service to Forfar was also provided, branching off the main line at Broughty Junction, but this ran for the last time in January 1955. *W. S. Sellar*

Dundee East

137 Class C16 No. 67496 enter Dundee East on 1st November 1958 charge of a four-coach local working. T East Coast main line is on a lower lev behind the retaining wall on the right the picture, having commenced its sha 1 in 60 descent into Dock Street tunr from Camperdown Junction signal box the background. *W. S. Sell*

138 Once the main line has emerged from the dark depths of Dock Street tunnel and passed Camperdown Junction, it then runs through the docks area. Most places where docks are situated tend to be dreary, and Dundee is no exception. An assortment of drab warehouse buildings and factories border the railway on both sides for the next mile or so. At one time a network of tracks laid along adjacent roads served the quaysides and local factories and diminutive *ex*-NBR Class Y9 0-4-0 saddle tank locomotives could be seen sedately pottering along with a string of wagons in tow. When this picture of Class A3 No. 60100, *Spearmint,* hauling the 12.30pm Aberdeen to Edinburgh train, was taken on 11th July 1964 the steam dock shunters were a thing of the past, though a line of tank wagons, just discernible in the distance, at least indicate the dock lines themselves were still in use at this time. *D. Hume*

39 'Broughty Ferry' proclaims a rather weather-beaten sign on the station's own platform, as the 2.15pm Dundee ast-Arbroath train rolls in behind one of ay Bridge shed's complement of Class 16 tank locomotives, No. 67486. This hotograph was taken on 5th April 958. *P. Hay*

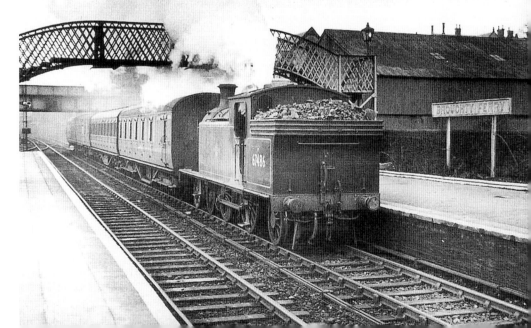

140 The photographer appears to have been very lucky to get this picture, the d.m.u. on the adjacent track having just cleared in the ni[ck] of time. The train is the 1.30pm Dundee to Montrose freight between Broughty Ferry and Monifieth on 22nd June 1966. The bridge in t[he] background used to carry the former CR line to Forfar. Motive power is provided by Class J37 No. 64602. *J. G. Mallinso[n]*

141 A local working bound for Dund[ee] East sets off from Carnoustie on 8th August 1956 hauled by Class C16 N[o]. 67490. *W. S. Sel[lar]*

142 A presentably-clean Class 5, No. 44794, leaves Carnoustie on 25th June 1966 with the 11.0am from Glasgow Buchanan Street to Aberdeen via Dundee. Constructed at Horwich Works in Lancashire, this locomotive was in traffic for almost twenty years, from August 1947 to April 1967.   *W. A. C. Smith*

143 Just a mile or so south of Arbroath station there is a small miniature railway which runs parallel with the main line for a short distance. It is the only location in Great Britain known to the author where this occurs. Kerr's Miniature Railway was founded in 1935 by Matthew Kerr and has reportedly carried more than a million and a half passengers since, and is increasing in popularity. This photograph, taken in April 1957, shows the driver of KMR No. 9872(!) waving to his counterpart on the footplate of a passing Class B1 4-6-0, No. 61278.   *W. S. Sellar*

144 The 5.17pm Arbroath to Dundee East train, hauled by Class C16 No. 67502, is seen just half a mile or so south o Arbroath station on 5th April 1958. Note the locomotive has its class and owning depot stencilled on its buffer beam.

P. Ho

145 Class V2 No. 60823 pulls awa from Arbroath with a southbound trai on 30th June 1958. The signal bo partially hidden by the second coach Arbroath South, while the statio frontage is just visible above the bridg parapet. Note the mixed liveries of th coaches forming the train. At that tim the old carmine and cream colou scheme was being phased out in favou of lined maroon, hence the mixture The splendid array of signals will also b noted; unusually the posts, which appl to the down line, are positioned on th up side of the line, presumably t improve sighting for engine crews.

W. S. Sell

146 Like Dundee Tay Bridge, Arbroath station is also a somewhat gloomy place, situated mostly in a cutting with a road overbridge and the station buildings above the platforms. The station frontage, part of which is visible here, is pleasant enough, however, and has the date of its construction (1911) cut into its stonework. Note the gas lighting, which was for so long a feature of many British stations. This picture, taken on 2nd May 1959, depicts Class A2 Pacific No. 60525, *A. H. Peppercorn,* waiting to depart with the 9.18am Aberdeen to Kings Cross train. *D. Hume*

Arbroath

riginally Arbroath was served by two stations, the terminus of the Dundee and Arbroath Railway was at Lady Loan while the rbroath and Forfar Railway passenger service, opened in 1838, terminated at Catherine Street, although there was a short ntinuation to the harbour for goods traffic only. Both lines were built to the 5ft 6in gauge and were connected by a single-ack horse-operated line through the streets of the town. The rapid expansion of railways in the early 1840s caused the two urely local lines to quickly emerge as a vital link in the national railway system connecting Aberdeen, Dundee and termediate towns with Perth and the south. In 1845 it was agreed between all interested parties that both routes would dergo conversion to standard gauge and a direct connection would be provided at Arbroath. The former was completed by ugust 1847 while the Arbroath 'connection' opened for freight in December 1847 and passenger operation two months er. The two independent terminus stations were closed at the same time, as a new through station was constructed to serve e town.

47 The northern end of Arbroath tion is not nearly so drab as the uthern end, as can be seen in this ew of the empty stock of an broath to Dundee East local train tering on 5th April 1958. The otive power is a Class C16, but this occasion the locomotive, . 67486, is in very clean ndition. These machines never d to exert themselves on this ute, the line being level apart m short gradients at each end.
P. Hay

148 Formed almost entirely of *ex*-LNER rolling stock, t[...] 11.0am Kings Cross to Aberdeen leaves Arbroath on 27[...] June 1964 headed by Class V2 No. 60816.

D. Hur[...]

149 An extremely dirty Class B1 4-6-0, No. 61347, pounds up the 1 in 100 bank north of Arbroath with a Dundee to Aberdeen freight [...] June 1964. After a very easy start to the journey from Dundee along level track, the B1's crew will have their work cut out for t[...] remainder of the trip as there are hardly any level stretches of line which exceed a mile in length. *D. Hum[...]*

150 Towards the end of steam it was always sad to see a once proud express passenger locomotive ekeing out a precarious existence on freight or van trains. One such example is seen here on 5th August 1965, but at least the engine is still doing revenue earning duties, even if working a train of cement wagons does not have quite the prestige of an East Coast express. The scene is the site of Lunan Bay station, which was one of a number of wayside stations between Arbroath and Montrose closed as long ago as September 1930. Sadly, the locomotive, No. 60027, *Merlin,* is in filthy external condition typical of St. Rollox-based engines during the mid-1960s.

John Goss

151 Lunan Bay is an attractive spot which so far seems to have successfully resisted any kind of development – you will not find any oil platforms or beach huts there, only peace and solitude. Perhaps this was not entirely true in the mid-1960s, however, when one of Dundee shed's Class J37 0-6-0s was venturing north on a freight working. These trains attracted many photographers anxious to capture the veteran J37s on film before it was too late, and here No. 64576 is pictured crossing Lunan Bay viaduct with the 1.30pm Dundee to Montrose freight on 19th July 1966.

C. E. Weston

153 Class V2 2-6-2 No. 60818 disturbs the peace of a Sunday evening as it climbs away from Montrose at the head of the 6.0pm SuO Aberdeen to Glasgow train on 29th August 1965. The author experienced a memorable journey on this train behind sister engine No. 60919 a week earlier. The stretch of water in the background is Montrose basin, a tidal lagoon through which the River South Esk flows out to the sea. *D. E. Gouldthorp*

152 *Opposite:* Class J37 No. 64547, presumably smartened up by enthusiasts, makes a pleasing sight as it purposefully climbs the taxing 1 in 88 gradient from Montrose to Usan signal box with the 5.5pm freight to Dundee on 18th July 1966. Looking at the twisting single line, which is composed of old bullhead track, it is difficult to believe that this is actually part of the East Coast main line and not a country branch. *C. E. Weston*

154 This is the southernmost of two viaducts which span the channels of Montrose basin where it flows out to the North Sea. The houses on the far side are actually on a small island between the two channels. Here the 5.5pm freight to Dundee is seen leaving Montrose behind No. 64576 on 19th July 1966. *C. E. Weston*

155 A CR 0-4-4T No. 55200, allocated to Forfar shed, simmers in a bay platform at Montrose on 12th July 1952, with the 12.20pm to Brechin, just a few weeks before this service ceased to operate on 4th August. This train will have run along former NBR metals for a short distance before branching off the main line to reach former CR territory at Broomfield Road Junction. From there the train will have passed underneath the East Coast main line, and soon afterwards reached Dubton Junction from where it is a direct run to Bridge of Dun and Brechin. The nine-mile journey occupied thirty eight minutes due to the train being detained at Bridge of Dun in order to connect with the 10.0am Glasgow-Aberdeen express. No. 55200 was very nearly destroyed in a fire at Montrose LMSR shed in May 1939. The conflagration was alleged to have been started by a night cleaner, but he redeemed himself by removing the two occupants before the flames caused any serious damage. *J. L. Stevenson*

Montrose

156 A supermarket car park now occupies the site of Montrose shed which is seen here in March 1967, on the occasion of one of the final steam-worked freight trains to Brechin. The Class J37 0-6-0 locomotive, No. 64611, was cleaned by visiting enthusiasts. The last steam working on the Brechin branch was widely expected to operate on 31st March but there was a problem with the substitute diesel locomotive during the following week, and the last steam working, using No. 64611, actually took place on the 7th April. Montrose Basin is visible in the distance. *M. S. Burn*

157 A work-stained J37, No. 64576, stands inside the gloomy interior of Montrose shed on 25th August 1966. *I. S. Krause*

158 Former NBR Class J37 0-6-0 No. 64615 poses at the site of the old CR Montrose station on 16th June 1960. The locomotive had just been detached from a rail tour, and was about to run round before proceeding to Inverbervie. The CR station at Montrose was closed to passengers as long ago as 1934, but subsequently remained in use for freight purposes for many years. The tour was not a one day jaunt of the type common today, but a small part of a comprehensive week-long trip organised jointly by two societies. The tour covered many lines in eastern Scotland which are now but a memory.

T. J. Edgington

Montrose first appeared on the railway map in February 1848 when a branch from Bridge of Dun to Rotten Row station, Montrose, was opened by the Aberdeen Railway. The fact that the Aberdeen Railway was involved may at first appear strange, but is explained by its desire – indeed necessity – to get at least a section of its proposed line southwards from the Granite City into operation and earning revenue as soon as possible. At this time the Aberdeen Railway was in a parlous financial condition due to an economic recession and the heavy expenditure incurred on civil engineering works. Actually, the branch continued from Bridge of Dun to Guthrie, where a triangular junction was made with the Arbroath and Forfar Railway. In addition a branch connected Bridge of Dun and Brechin. So, passengers from Montrose could reach Brechin, Forfar, Arbroath and Dundee over the Aberdeen Railway's (and associated companies') tracks, but not at this stage Aberdeen itself, which was reached by horse drawn coach from Brechin and Montrose. It is recorded, however, that many of the stations were incomplete without proper access roads or goods sheds, and at Montrose the make-shift terminus was so badly situated that a horse-drawn coach was laid on to the town centre! The next development in the area was the opening of the Aberdeen Railway's section of line from Dubton Junction, just outside Montrose, to Limpet Mill, north of Stonehaven, which occurred on 1st November 1849. The Aberdeen Railway's separate existence as an independent company ended in 1856 when it merged with the Scottish Midland Junction Railway to form the Scottish North Eastern Railway. Before this it achieved its goal of reaching Aberdeen from the south, the route opening in 1850, despite financial problems. In 1865 a branch from Montrose to Bervie was eventually opened by a local company following the withdrawal from the scene of the Great North of Scotland Railway (GNSR), which had envisaged the Bervie branch as part of its own independent route to the south.

The next major railway development in the area was the construction of a direct line from Montrose to Arbroath, by the NBR. The citizens of Montrose were frustrated by the town's lowly position at the end of a CR branch line from Bridge of Dun and wished to achieve main line status. The preliminary prospectus for the sixteen miles-long line was issued in February 1871 and, as might be expected, it enjoyed massive local support with many local dignitaries actively promoting the proposed new line. It was opened in stages for goods traffic only, with passenger services – for local travellers only at first – being introduced from 1st March 1881. Just over two years later the first through express trains from the south to Aberdeen were operated. It is often said that the last railways to be built were invariably the first to close. This rule certainly does not apply to the Arbroath – Montrose line which today is the only route connecting Aberdeen with the south, and appears to have a very secure future as part of the East Coast Main Line.

159 Complete closure of the Inverbervie branch took place on 22nd May 1966, in a blaze of glory. Two packed six-coach special trains were run from Montrose, which were apparently organised by a local lady. Class J37 No. 64547, suitably spruced up for the occasion, was provided as motive power. The first trip left Montrose at 1.30pm, while the final train departed at 5.0pm On the first trip a 350hp diesel shunter was provided as banker as far as Johnshaven, but despite the heavy rain the train had little difficulty with the steep grades, and in fact as it crossed North Water viaduct (at the start of two miles at 1 in 50) the shunter was about a coach length behind the train! The second trip was unassisted. Here the J37 is seen approaching Broomfield Junction with the last train.

J. Dagley-Morris

Inverbervie Branch

160 The first train is seen crossing North Water viaduct on its way back to Montrose. The closure caught the imagination of the local people who turned out in force to witness the events. An archway of bunting and flags was reportedly erected over the line near Broomfield Junction.

J. Dagley-Morris

161 The well-preserved station at Johnshaven appeared to be in use as a residence when No. 64608 paused there *en route* back from Inverbervie to Montrose on 5th August 1965. Note the track does not appear to have seen the weed-killing train for some time!

John Goss

A line from Montrose to Bervie was first proposed in 1860, but difficulty was experienced in raising the necessary capital. The Great North of Scotland Railway (GNSR) which at that time was fiercely independent and wished to obtain its own route southwards bought a large financial holding in the Montrose and Bervie Railway on the understanding that the local company would seek powers to extend its line northwards for ten miles from Bervie to Stonehaven and southwards for fourteen miles from Montrose to Arbroath. These plans were, however, thwarted by Parliament and the GNSR later disposed of its financial stake in the Bervie line leaving the purely local company to finance the construction. The railway, which was single throughout, was opened on 1st November 1865, and was worked by the Scottish North Eastern Railway, which had been formed in 1856. In 1872 a connection was authorised between the NBR's proposed Arbroath – Kinnaber Junction line and Broomfield Junction, where the Bervie Railway diverged from the CR's Montrose branch. A passenger station, known as Broomfield Road Junction, was provided at this location for a short time. The signalbox here was unlucky enough to be struck by a aircraft during the last war and suffered severe damage: it was later rebuilt. Bervie Station was renamed Inverbervie in 1926. The branch passenger service ran for the last time in October 1951, and the line closed to all traffic in 1966.

162 Class J37 No. 64624 pulls away from Inverbervie with the return daily pick-up goods working on 16th July 1964. Just over a year previously the infamous Beeching Report on the future of the railways had been published and one of its top priorities was the elimination of this type of uneconomic goods working which, in the case of this delightful backwater, was achieved within two years. *M. Mensing*

163 A peaceful scene at Inverbervie on 6th July 1964 as the crew of No. 64558 take a rest while the train is loaded. A small boy stands on the platform admiring the elderly, but rather dirty, Class J37. *M. Mensing*

164 The 1.30pm Aberdeen t
Glasgow train, headed by N
60532, *Blue Peter*, is seen durir
the summer of 1966 passing Log
which is a small hamlet situate
between Kinnaber Junction and tl
former Craigo station, a victim (
the June 1956 closures. The train
crossing a bridge which carries tl
line across a tributary of the Riv
North Esk.   *M. S. Burn*

165 The 1.30pm from Aberdeen is seen again, this time pausing at Laurencekirk behind Class 5 No. 44704 on 10th July 1965. Th
station seems deserted, apart from two gentlemen who appear to be railway staff, so perhaps the decision to close the station, at the sam
time as the Strathmore route, on 4th September 1967, was justified. The goods yard, situated at the north end of the northbound platform
is concealed by the footbridge. Note the attractive flower beds, and generally tidy condition of the station.   *D. Hum*

66 On 18th July 1966 No. 60532, *Blue Peter,* nears Carmont with 'The Grampian', the 1.30pm ex-Aberdeen.   *J. G. Mallinson*

Climbing to Carmont

67 Class A4 Pacific No. 60034 *Lord Faringdon,* climbs the last mile to Carmont summit with the 1.30pm ex-Aberdeen in May 1966. Notice there are at least two enthusiasts leaning from the windows of the leading coach. In today's modern world this, admittedly hazardous, pastime is frowned upon by the authorities. Window bars have been fitted to vehicles regularly employed on rail tours, while most modern air-conditioned stock has no opening windows at all!

C. E. Weston

168 After four miles of continuou climbing, mostly at 1 in 102, fror Stonehaven, Class A4 No. 60019 *Bittern,* has steam to spare as it near the summit of the climb at Carmon The train is the 5.15pm Aberdeen t Glasgow, 'The Granite City', and th photograph was taken in May 1966.
C. E. Westo

169 On 20th March 1965 Class 5 No. 45013 is seen hard at work lifting the 1.30pm *ex*-Aberdeen up the 1 in 102 gradient betwee Stonehaven and Carmont. This little-known spot, which can only be reached on foot across open fields from the nearest road, is about fou miles from Stonehaven, and one mile from the summit. The bridge carries the railway across the Carron Water which flows into the Nort Sea at Stonehaven. Since this photograph was taken mature trees have developed in this area, completely obliterating the view of th railway as seen here.
C. E. Westo

170 Photographed at another location well off the beaten track Class A4 Pacific No. 60034, *Lord Faringdon,* is seen climbing to Carmont with 'The Grampian', 1.30pm from Aberdeen, on a freezing day in February 1966. The distinctive stone bridge in this picture carries the railway over the Carron Water. Heavy afforestation has since occurred along this section of line, making this view virtually unrecognisable today. *C. E. Weston*

171 Proving that a view of a train descending from the summit is just as interesting as a picture of one going up the bank, this is the 11.0am Glasgow to Aberdeen drifting down to Stonehaven behind Class B1 4-6-0 No. 61263 on 9th July 1966. This is another location which can only be reached on foot, and in this case the efforts of the photographer have been rewarded with a very attractive picture. The stream visible on the right is the Carron Water which the railway parallels for most of the way to Stonehaven.

D. E. Gouldthorp

172 Looking in the other direction from the vantage point of the previous photograph, a BR Standard 2-6-4T locomotive, No. 80090, is seen purposefully climbing the bank with a single brake van in tow on 20th March 1965. This machine was withdrawn from service the following week, so this may have been its last journey – presumably to its home depot of Dundee Tay Bridge. *C. E. Weston*

Stonehaven

173 In the days long before the appearance of *Bittern* and *Lord Faringdon* on the line, the 5.30pm Aberdeen to Glasgow train pauses at Stonehaven on 6th September 1948. Two spotlessly clean former LMSR locomotives, 'Compound' 4-4-0 No. 41176 and Class 5 No. 44999, provide the motive power for the uniform rake of *ex*-LMSR coaches in early BR carmine and cream livery. At that time a 'Compound' was regularly provided by Forfar shed to assist the 10.0am *ex*-Buchanan Street to Aberdeen, returning as pilot on the 5.30pm Aberdeen to Glasgow. *J. L. Stevenson*

174 A northbound freight hauled by Class WD 2-8-0 No. 90168 approaches Stonehaven in 1965. The brilliant low sun illuminates the locomotive excellently, but fails to find any clean paintwork on which to reflect. *C. E. Weston*

175 Stonehaven station lies in a dip, and therefore trains starting away are faced with adverse gradients in both directions. Southbound trains face the more strenuous climb, but those going north have to contend with two miles of gradients varying between 1 in 100 and 1 in 160. Here, the 11.0am Glasgow-Aberdeen is pictured on 23rd July 1966 storming up the stiff climb behind Class B1 No. 61102. BR Standard coaches make up the train, apart from the vehicle immediately behind the locomotive which is of LMSR origin. *John Goss*

176 Class A4 No. 60027, *Merlin,* crosses Glenury Viaduct with a train of empty cement wagons returning to Dunbar from Aberdeen in March 1965. The viaduct, which is situated about half a mile north of Stonehaven station, carries the railway across the Cowie Water. No. 60027 was one of two A4s – the other was No. 60031, *Golden Plover* – disfigured by a yellow diagonal stripe on the cabsides, which denoted locomotives banned from working south of Crewe(!) due to restricted overhead live wire clearances. This was apparently carried out at the insistence of the LMR because those two engines sometimes worked into Carlisle on Waverley route freight trains. No. 60027 entered traffic in March 1937, and spent the first twenty-five years of its career at Edinburgh Haymarket shed. In May 1962 it was moved to St. Rollox for use on the three-hour trains to Aberdeen. It was sent back to Edinburgh – though now based at St. Margarets shed – for the final year of its service, and was withdrawn in September 1965. In 1946 it was embellished with a crest from HMS Merlin which was carried on the boiler-side casing. *C. E. Weston*

177 For most of the journey north of Stonehaven the railway is within sight of the rugged coastline, and the North Sea is rarely out of view. On 28th December 1965 Class A4 No. 60024, *Kingfisher,* is pictured between Muchalls and Stonehaven hauling the 1.30pm Aberdeen to Glasgow train, with a light dusting of snow adding interest to the scene. *M. S. Burns*

178 On 25th March 1967 an ambitious rail tour was organised by the Scottish Region which was steam-hauled over the Perth to Aberdeen portion, via the Strathmore route. Formed of a mammoth load of eighteen coaches the train started from Edinburgh, and was diesel-hauled over the Waverley route to Carlisle. The special then returned north with the same motive power to Perth, where Class 5 No. 44997, piloting A4 No. 60009, *Union of South Africa,* took over for the run to Aberdeen. A brilliant run ensued with the 89¾ miles between those points being covered at an average speed of 61.8mph. After this excitement the train continued northwards to Keith and eventually gained Aviemore, using diesel traction. After a trip along the Highland main line to Perth, the Class 5 and A4 again took charge, returning the marathon excursionists to Edinburgh. Amazingly, the fare for the tour was only fifty shillings (£2.50p). The train is pictured north of Stonehaven.

M. S. Burns

179 In pouring rain 'The Grampian', 1.30pm *ex*-Aberdeen, approaches Muchalls on 23rd May 1966 behind Class A2 No. 60528, *Tudor Minstrel.* This machine was normally employed on 'stand by' duties at Dundee Tay Bridge shed at this period so its movements were, to say the least, unpredictable. As far as the author is aware No. 60528 was never regularly employed on the Glasgow-Aberdeen service during 1966, so it would seem the photographer was very fortunate indeed to obtain this rare shot. *J. Dagley-Morris*

180 The scene is at Newtonhill viaduct, about seven miles north of Stonehaven, on 30th May 1966, with Class A4 No. 60019, *Bittern*, racing along at the head of the 8.25am from Glasgow to Aberdeen. The viaduct carries the railway across the Burn of Elsick which meets the sea at Newtonhill harbour which is less than a mile from where this photograph was taken. There used to be a station at Newtonhill, but this was closed in June 1956.

C. E. Weston

181 The up 'West Coast Postal', in charge of Class A4 No. 60016, *Silver King*, races through the former Portlethen station on a dull 16th May 1964. There is a brief downhill stretch in favour of southbound trains, before the station, but the line starts to climb again just before the station is reached. This adverse gradient is quite short, with most of the grades over the next few miles to Stonehaven favouring trains heading south. Portlethen station has been reopened principally to serve new housing development in the area.

D. Hume

Climbing past Cove Bay

182 A southbound freight with Class V2 2-6-2 No. 60844 in charge makes a fine sight as it plods up the 1 in 116 gradient near Cove Bay on 15th July 1965. Trains going south from Aberdeen have to contend with seven miles of adverse grades mostly at 1 in 150 or thereabouts until the summit is reached a mile from Portlethen. *S. C. Nash*

183 Another southbound freight, this time headed by Class V2 No. 60818 makes a stirring sight – and no doubt sound as well – as it climbs past Cove Bay. The deep rock cutting at this point gives some idea of the problems encountered when this section of line was constructed.   *M. S. Burns*

184 Class A2 Pacific No. 60525, *A. H. Peppercorn,* skirts the coastline near Nigg Bay with the 7.5pm to Kings Cross on 3rd July 1958. The first vehicle is most unusual; it is designated a restaurant car, but also has a guard's brake van and is articulated into the bargain! This must be one of the few locations in Great Britain where a main line runs in close proximity to a lighthouse, which provides a most distinctive background.   *P. J. Shoesmith*

185 The 10.10am Aberdeen to London Euston heads out of the Granite City on 15th July 1965 hauled by Class 5 No. 44703. The train was photographed passing Nigg Bay, which is out of the picture on the right.   *S. C. Nash*

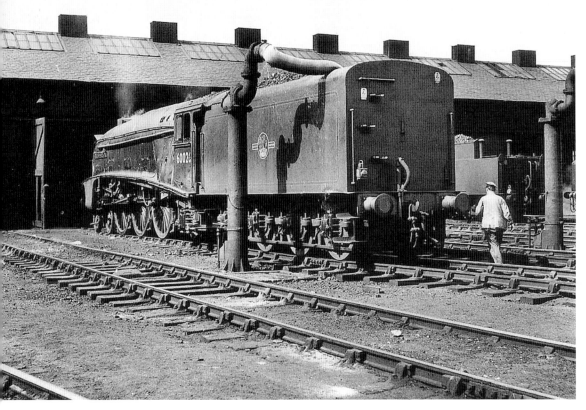

186 Class A4 No. 60026, *Miles Beevor,* takes water outside Ferryhill shed on 5th June 1965 before going off shed for main line duty. The building seen here dates from 1908 when a new twelve-road shed was constructed, including two bays in a separate repair and machine shop. A seventy feet-long turntable was provided. This shed replaced earlier premises which had proved inadequate. In the early days the shed was shared by the CR and NBR and this gave rise to endless disputes regarding operating expenses and suchlike. Ferryhill's allocation was always modest for a shed of such size, perhaps because so much of the motive power for trains to the south was provided by other depots, notably Perth. Following closure to steam traction in March 1967 it continued in use as a diesel depot; the building was still standing, albeit in dilapidated condition, twenty-five years later. *Martin S. Welch*

Aberdeen Ferryhill Shed

187 Class A4 No. 60024, *Kingfisher,* is seen undergoing minor repairs to its motion inside Ferryhill shed sometime during 1966.

C. E. Weston

188 *Above:* Three giants of steam! A trio of A4s, Nos. 60009/24/34, enjoy the hospitality of Ferryhill shed during a night in February 1966.   *C. E. Weston*

189 Another shot of the same machines with Nos. 60009, *Union of South Africa,* and 60024, *Kingfisher,* nearest the camera. The popularity of the Class A4s is such that at least three railway publishers have adopted the names of members of the class.   *C. E. Weston*

190 'Princess Royal' Pacific No. 46210 *Lady Patricia,* in blue livery, approaches Ferryhill in the early 1950s with the southbound 'West Coast Postal'. This impressive locomotive was constructed in 1935, and was among the first members of its class to be withdrawn, in October 1961. *P. J. Lynch*

Construction of the remaining section of the Aberdeen Railway's line into the city was beset with problems, due to lack of funds and difficulty in finding a suitable station site in Aberdeen. During 1848 the railway was gripped by a financial crisis and work all but came to a halt on some sections of the line between Stonehaven and Aberdeen. The company needed £300,000 to complete the line and it was only after a new appeal to shareholders that the necessary capital was eventually raised, and work could resume with increased vigour. On 13th December 1849 a goods service started from Portlethen to the south, with passenger trains commencing operation a few months later. A daily goods train to London reached the English capital within twenty-four hours.

The problem of acquiring a site for a station in Aberdeen proved a major headache, principally due to opposition from within the city itself. Initially, a site on the south bank of the River Dee was considered, but this would have been very inconvenient for passengers, and in any case the Aberdeen Railway had already built a substantial stone bridge across the river. In the end, the railway took its tracks across the river and opened a temporary station at Ferryhill, from which full public services commenced on 1st April 1850. Four months later the line was extended to a new station at Guild Street, much nearer the city centre.

The progress of the AR stimulated interest in a route running north from the city, and a Great North scheme had been put forward as early as 1845. It was the intention to connect Aberdeen with Inverness via the small market town of Huntly. Despite Parliamentary approval being given to the Aberdeen to Huntly section in 1846, difficulty was experienced in raising the necessary capital, with the result that the line did not open until September 1854. Four years later the line was completed through to Inverness.

The Great North of Scotland Railway's terminus at Kittybrewster was a mile from the city centre and through passengers had to find their own way from one station to the other. A branch was opened for goods traffic to Waterloo in September 1855 and this at least provided an opportunity for the transfer of goods between the AR and the GNSR using tracks in the harbour area. This ridiculous situation gave rise to a proposal in 1861 for the construction of a new line which would by-pass Aberdeen altogether. This was intended to connect Limpet Mill (three miles north of Stonehaven) with the GNSR line at Kintore, but nothing came of these plans.

Pressure for a proper connection between the two systems serving Aberdeen came from the local traders, however, and despite the antagonism the two railways had for each other, a scheme for a new joint station was eventually agreed. This involved a new piece of line, including the boring of two tunnels between the new station and former GNSR terminus at Kittybrewster. The joint station was opened on 4th November 1867 and at last Aberdeen had a unified railway system. The new station was soon found to be inadequate and after various wrangles between the two companies agreement was reached on replacement in 1899. It was not until after the First World War that the project was completed.

191 On 27th April 1958, Class A2 No. 60528, *Tudor Minstrel,* approaches Ferryhill Junction in charge of a southbound express. *W. S. Sellar*

192 Class A4 No. 60034, *Lord Faringdon,* brightens an otherwise typically dull and wet mid-winter's afternoon as it charges out of Aberdeen with the 1.30pm departure to Glasgow on 28th January 1966.   *D. E. Gouldthorp*

193 Class A4 No. 60011, *Empire of India,* passes Aberdeen South signal box as it leaves the Granite City with a Glasgow-bound train in 1962. This signal box, like others in the city, was made redundant by a resignalling scheme, this particular box being closed in August 1981. Apart from a short spell at Kings Cross shed immediately after entering traffic in June 1937, No.60011 spent its entire working life at Haymarket shed until transfer to Ferryhill took place in June 1962. It was a regular performer on the three-hour Glasgow services until March 1964 when it hit the buffer stops at Buchanan Street station. It was sent to Darlington Works for repair but was condemned, and broken-up there in July 1964.

P. J. Lynch

194 In this flashback to the mid-1950s, Class D34 4-4-0 No. 62482, *Glen Mamie,* is seen standing at the south end of Aberdeen station with a freight working. This photograph was taken on 11th August 1954. *P. Hay*

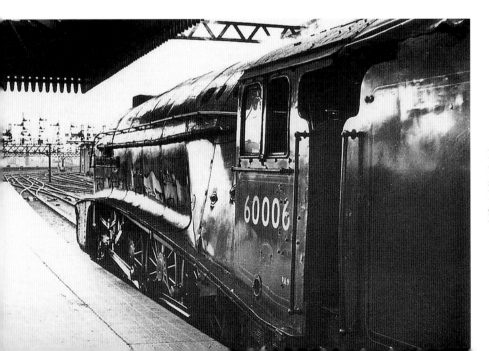

195 An immaculately clean A4 Pacific, No.60006, *Sir Ralph Wedgwood,* waits for the road prior to departure with a southbound train sometime in 1965. Note the impressive array of signal gantries which were such a distinctive feature of the railway scene at Aberdeen. *M. S. Burns*

196 Two small boys gaze up in awe at the fireman of Class A3 No. 60052, *Prince Palatine,* as it awaits departure from Aberdeen with the 12.30pm to Edinburgh Waverley on 4th July 1964. This locomotive survived in service until January 1966, and was the last of its class in traffic.   *W. A. C. Smith*

Journey's end – Aberdeen, The Granite City

197 A sad moment at Aberdeen as No. 60019, *Bittern,* awaits the 'right away' with a special train returning to Glasgow on September 3rd 1966. This was one of the commemorative specials organised by the Scottish Region and advertised as 'the last public run behind an A4'. The trains made the journey in three hours, with the usual intermediate stops, and all this for a fare of £2! Whilst the locomotive was being serviced, Ferryhill shed was specially opened to visitors, and sister locomotives Nos. 60009 and 60024 were positioned for photography. In the event, however, *Bittern*'s runs on 3rd September did not prove to be the last Class A4 trips along the route as *Kingfisher* worked the 6.30am Perth to Aberdeen local train the following week. The real finale took place the week after when *Kingfisher* worked the 5.15pm from Aberdeen to Glasgow on 13th September, returning home for the last time at the head of the 8.25am from Buchanan Street the following day, thus closing a glorious chapter in the history of the Glasgow to Aberdeen route.   *D. Hume*

C.E. Weston

Acknowledgement

I would like to record my appreciation to all the steam enthusiasts who have assisted with the compilation of this album. Tony Davies has undertaken considerable research in order to produce an informative account of the four and a half year reign of the Class A4 'Pacifics' on the Aberdeen road and dug into his archives to unearth a number of logs of the locomotives' performance. Much of the historical information used in the book was obtained from a variety of material held in the collections of Terence A. Barry and Graham Burtenshaw. A number of gentlemen read through the original manuscript and suggested alterations which I feel have greatly improved the end result. In this connection I am indebted to Chris Evans, David J. Fakes, John J. Smith and James Stevenson. I must not overlook Kemi Sotinwa who made an excellent job of typing the manuscript. Stephen Mourton, of Runpast Publishing, has given me a free hand regarding the content and layout of the book: any errors which have crept in are entirely my responsibility. I must not, of course, forget to thank the very large number of photographers who responded to my request for illustrations. Many were kind enough to lend their irreplaceable original negatives from which Derek Mercer has produced prints of the highest quality. The largest single photographic contribution has been provided by Douglas Hume who was able to submit a wide selection of views of the Glasgow to Aberdeen line including some rarely photographed locations. The following list of photographers includes all those who offered material, although not everybody was fortunate when the final selection was made. My thanks are due to: David Anderson, Maurice Burns, David Clark, David Cross, John Dagley-Morris, John Edgington, John Everitt, Ken Falconer, John Goss, David E. Gouldthorp, Peter Hay, Roy Hobbs, Douglas Hume, Ian Krause, Paul Leavens, Rodney Lissenden, Phil Lynch, Graham Mallinson, Michael Mensing, Gavin Morrison, Sid Nash, Les Nixon, Norman Preedy, John Price, Stuart Sellar, Peter Shoesmith, John J. Smith, W.A.C. Smith, Tim Stephens, James Stevenson, Philip Wells, Martin Welch, Chris Weston, John Whiteley, Martin Wilkins, Edwin Wilmshurst and Derek Winkworth.

Bibliography

LMS Engine Sheds, Volume Five
Chris Hawkins and George Reeve,
Wild Swan Publications

LMS Engines. J.W.P. Rowledge
David and Charles 1989

A Regional History of the Railways of Great Britain
Volume Six, John Thomas, David and Charles, 1971
Volume Fifteen, John Thomas and David Turnock,
David and Charles 1989

Yeadons Register of LNER Locomotives:
Volume 2 Gresley A4 and W1 Classes
W.B. Yeadon, Irwell Press.

The Railways of Brechin. W. Simms
Angus District Libraries and Museums, 1985

Passengers No More. Gerald Daniels and Les Dench
Ian Allan, 1980

Various editions of *The Railway Magazine* and *The Railway Observer* have also proved valuable sources of material.